The Royal House of Tudor

CLXX

The Royal House of Tudor

Michael Roulstone

CLXX

A Balfour Book printed and published by
Photo Precision Ltd., St. Ives, Huntingdon, Cambridgeshire, England.

FIRST EDITION 1974

ISBN 0 85944 005 2

Printed and published in Great Britain by
Balfour Publications (Photo Precision Ltd.)
St. Ives, Huntingdon, Cambridgeshire, England.

Contents

Contents cont.

Foreword

'The Royal House of Tudor' embraces the period between 1485 and 1603. It does not aim to present formal history, but rather a scrap-book of the age reflecting the influences and activities of the Crown, its ministers and associates. With the aid of lavish illustration, the greater part of it in colour and most of it taken from contemporary sources, the book presents a panorama of a dynasty.

The text outlines various aspects of the Tudor reign, divided into a series of convenient sections. The illustrations supplement this; but also they constitute an individual part of the book, supported by sometimes extended captions. From these illustrations, without the necessity for copious explanation, the reader will find it possible to learn much more about many aspects of life in the Tudor period. The book is in fact something of an anthology, both of words and illustrations.

The political history of these years is full of excitement, ranging from warfare to intrigue, from treason to heresy. The cultural aspect of Tudor times embraces the flowering of drama and the sudden invigoration of both pictorial and musical art forms. Publishing all at once became a flourishing business proposition. Colonisation and commerce introduced new vistas to the English way of life. All of these matters are touched upon; but by and large the main stress has been placed on the members of the royal family themselves, at least two of whom could arguably be defined as among the greatest English monarchs of all time: Henry VIII and Elizabeth I. Justly, more attention has been shown to their two long reigns than to those of the other members of the House of Tudor.

If any one concise assessment can be made of the achievement of the House of Tudor, it is that it represented the Renaissance spirit in England. It is hoped that this publication reflects this judgment.

Introduction—the Coming of the Tudors

The Tudors came from Wales and at the time of the future Henry VII's birth had been long established in and around Anglesey. None of them had, however, achieved any position of eminence until the emergence of Owen Tudor who became a Clerk of the Wardrobe to Henry V's widow, Catherine of France. By a process of ingratiation he eventually succeeded in winning the dowager queen's hand and having two sons by her — though the marriage was not publicly admitted until after Catherine's death in 1437. Then the match was declared to have been illegal and for two years Owen was obliged to languish in Newgate prison, twice escaping and eventually being pardoned.

Owen's next venture was to ally himself with the Lancastrians in their struggle against the Yorkists, but in this speculation too he proved less than lucky, and following the victory of the latter forces at the Battle of Mortimer's Cross on February 2, 1461 he was executed.

Owen's two sons prospered through the indulgence of their half brother, Henry VI, who created Jasper Earl of Pembroke and Edmund Earl of Richmond. It was in Pembroke that Edmund's wife, Margaret Beaufort, following the death of her husband, gave birth to the first monarch of the Tudor dynasty.

Margaret was herself of the House of York, and thus not only had the Tudors passed rapidly from one loyalty to another but they had attached themselves remarkably quickly to the ruling classes in England. The young Henry Tudor was brought up in Wales by his uncle Jasper, almost losing this uncle when Lord Herbert conquered the latter, causing uncle and nephew to flee for safety to Brittany — but not before Herbert had attempted unsuccessfully to arrange a match between Henry and his own daughter, Maud.

It was from Harfleur, on August 1, 1485, that Henry Tudor, the 'unknown Welshman' as Richard III described him, set sail on his quest for the English throne. He had no strong justification for wishing to become King of England, but he was the only direct descendant of the once ruling House of Lancaster. He had consolidated this association by betrothing himself to a daughter of York, to Elizabeth, daughter of Edward IV and sister of Edward V, whose mother enjoyed the title of Dowager Queen of England. But however an unlikely eventuality it might have appeared to observers at the time, his mission to England proved successful and he did assume the crown.

It was with the Battle of Bosworth Field and the death of Richard III, on August 22, 1485, that the close of the Middle Ages in England was heralded. Only life in the monasteries, many of which had been established since pre-Norman times, was to continue in the medieval way; and even that would vanish before long. With the ascendancy of the House of Tudor a truly new era was initiated. It was to culminate in the great might and affluence enjoyed by England during the reign of Elizabeth I, the last of the Tudor line.

Over the 118 years (1485-1603) embraced by the Tudor dynasty England experienced a multitude of shocks and changes: wars with France, Spain and Scotland; the severance of the Church from that of Rome; the dissolution of the monasteries; a large number of beheadings and burnings at the stake, of favourites, traitors, wives and 'heretics'; urgent quests to voyage, discover, colonise; the advance of printing and the spread of the printed word; a noteworthy flowering of the arts under Henry VIII and Elizabeth. These are

but a few of the events and circumstances glanced at in the following pages; while prominent men and women pass before us in great number: Thomas Cromwell, the Lord Protector Somerset, William Cecil, Sir Francis Drake, Sir Walter Raleigh, William Shakespeare and many more.

The background of the House of Tudor was humble, and it was destined to vanish at the death of Elizabeth I; but the achievement of England during the period of its ascendancy was remarkable. The wiliness and tenacity of purpose of the first of the Tudors was in a large measure responsible for much of this.

Part One

Henry VII

Henry VII assumes the Throne

And moreover, the king ascertaineth you that Richard, Duke of Gloucester, late called King Richard, was slain at a place called Sandford within the shire of Leicester, and brought dead off the field into the town of Leicester, and there laid openly, that every man might see and look upon him. And also there was slain upon the same field John, late Duke of Norfolk; John, late Earl of Lincoln; Thomas, late Earl of Surrey; Francis, Viscount Lovell; Sir Walter Deveres, Lord Ferrers; Richard Ratclyff, knight; Robert Brackenbury, knight; with many other knights, squires, and gentlemen. Of whose souls God have mercy.
(Proclamation of Henry VII, York, August 25, 1485).

Following the death of Richard III on Bosworth Field it is recorded that Henry Tudor fell to his knees and rendered thanks to God for his victory. At that precise moment there was no crown available to signify the conqueror's regnal assumption, for it had fallen from Richard's head and rolled beneath a bush. It was quickly recovered, somewhat the worse for having been worn by Richard in battle, and placed on Henry's head. In effect this constituted the first of the Tudors' 'coronation', ratification being contained in the immediate acclaim of his supporters and the subsequent demonstrations of approval that he met as he journeyed to London.

On October 30, 1485 Henry was formally crowned in London, the ceremony being both impressive and costly. Thereafter he quietly began to reward his followers, noble and humble alike, for their support. Stanley became the Earl of Derby and Pembroke the Duke of Bedford; but these were by no means the sole beneficiaries of his gratitude, and men in lowlier stations found themselves appointed to porterships in castles and keeperships of his royal hunting preserves. By means such as these Henry gradually ingratiated himself into the minds of Englishmen, establishing what was to prove a lasting supremacy. He further enjoyed the by no means insignificant advantage of most of his earlier opponents having been slain in battle — Norfolk, Brackenbury, Catesby and others.

In order to overcome the ambiguity of a man who had previously been accounted an outlaw now enjoying power and popularity, Henry caused a simple act of parliament to be passed: '. . . be it ordained established and enacted by authority of the present parliament, that the inheritance of the crowns of the realms of England and France . . . be, rest, and remain and abide in the most royal person of our new Sovereign Lord King Henry the VIIth and in the heirs of his body lawfully comen perpetually'. Then, in order further to ensure the acceptability of his position, Henry set about formally restoring to their rightful stations those among his supporters who had earlier lost them by power of attainder for following the then exiled Henry Tudor. This he effected by the simple process of causing parliament to declare that Henry had been king technically even at the time of the Battle of Bosworth and that power of attainder could not therefore have been applied to those who had never deserted the rightful monarch. To balance this example of legal jugglery he also restored certain of his enemies to their former possessions, freeing both the Earl of Northumberland and the Earl of Surrey from their imprisonment in the Tower.

Henry is generally taken to have been a parsimonious monarch. It has already been said that he spent lavishly on his coronation, buying rich cloth for

King Arthur's Round Table, Winchester Cathedral. With the accession of Henry Tudor, who claimed descent from the seventh century Welsh prince, Cadwaladr (who was often linked with the legendary Arthur), much play was made of the Arthurian cult, whose adherents held that Arthur in the form of a descendant would occupy the English throne once again. By encouraging this belief Henry hoped to justify his occupation of the English throne. This round table, with its Tudor 'rose of unity' at the centre, illustrates the seriousness with which the assertion was sometimes taken.

each of his numerous attendants, but this was certainly an exception to his general rule, intended to impress any who had not wholly accepted him. His personal household expenses were by no means high, and a fragment of document preserved in the Public Records Office sets them, all told, at £14,365 10s. 7d. annually, which provided for everything from the entertainment of foreign diplomats to the upkeep of the royal stables. Perhaps unexpectedly, this sum included an estimated £2,105 19s. 11d. as provision for the extensive royal wardrobe. Henry's carefulness over matters connected with his personal finances extended in many directions: one of the most vindictive of his measures in this direction was to forbid unauthorised hunting in royal forests, declaring the offence a felony.

Elizabeth of York

Although by this meanes al things seemed to be brought in good and perfect order, yet there lacked a wrest to the harpe, to set all the strings in a monacorde and perfecte tune, which was the matrimonie to be finished betwene the king and the Lady Elizabeth, daughter to king Edward, which like a good Prince,

In 1495 Sir William Stanley, who had rescued the fallen crown on Bosworth Field and placed it on Henry's head, was beheaded. Stanley, a member of his king's council, appointed Lord Chamberlain in 1485 and Great Master of the Household in 1490, was guilty of treason, having become what was rumoured to be the richest commoner in the realm, possessing a vast fortune and said to be enjoying an annual income of £3,000. Together with Sir Robert Clifford, Stanley was alleged to have been plotting Henry's downfall; his death had the additional advantage of adding riches to the king's exchequer. This illustration from Holinshed's Chronicles should not be regarded as an accurate representation of the occurrence, for it is employed in several places in the book in connection with other executions.

*according to his othe, & promise, did both solemnise & consummate shortely
after, that is to saye, on the xviii day of Januarie, by reason of whych marriage,
peace was thought to descende out of heaven into England, considering that the
lynes of Lancaster & Yorke were now brought into one knot, and cornered
togither, of whose two bodies, one heire myghte succeede to rule and enjoye the
whole monarchie and realme of Englande.*

(Holinshed's Chronicles).

Henry's marriage to Elizabeth Plantagenet of York was an extremely satisfactory move: not only was she the daughter of Edward IV and sister of the
short-reigning Edward V (1483), but her mother Elizabeth, Edward IV's
widow, had previously enjoyed the title of Dowager Queen of England and as
such she was the senior surviving member of the royal house of York. When he
restored their possessions to such men as Northumberland and Surrey,
therefore, Henry also allowed the older Elizabeth to re-assume her royal title.
By marrying her daughter he not only united the rival houses of York and
Lancaster, but also consolidated his own position as king. Before allowing the
marriage to take place, however, and to ensure that it did not appear simply a
political stroke, Henry made quite certain that his own popularity was fully
established.

As can be seen from Elizabeth's portrait, Henry's new queen was a very
attractive woman, quite appropriately referred to as the 'White Rose of York'.
She had actually been betrothed to Henry in 1483 while the latter was still Earl
of Richmond, but their marriage was not finally celebrated until January 18,
1486. To the alarm and disapproval of her family her coronation was then
deferred until November 25, 1488. Thereafter Elizabeth Plantagenet's married
life was not, it would appear, completely satisfactory, the historian Francis
Bacon being enabled to write as follows: 'the King all his lifetime showed himself
no indulgent husband towards her; but that his aversion towards the house of
York was so predominant in him, as it found place not only in his wars and
councils, but also in his chamber and bed'. If this comment is to be accepted as
fact, Henry's determination when still Earl of Richmond appears all the more
pronounced.

LIZABETHA · VXOR
HENRICI · VII ·

Elizabeth bore Henry five children: Arthur, Henry, Margaret, Mary and Catherine; she died in the Tower of London on February 11, 1503, her forty first birthday, only nine days following the birth of her fifth child. Her marriage to Henry had been accompanied by all the trappings of papal approval, serving to strengthen Henry's assumption of might even further. But even in this matter Henry demonstrated how certain he was of his own position: for the marriage went ahead before Pope Innocent VIII's bull of March 27, 1486 could be issued. In this bull the Pope formally recognised Henry as the rightful King of England and threatened excommunication to any who might thenceforth oppose him.

Elizabeth's cannot have been an altogether happy existence. Her husband was frequently absent from court, while her particular duties as mother of the future king, Prince Arthur, were brought to an abrupt conclusion with the sickly young prince's death in Ludlow in 1502. A sad aspect of her life and premature death is comprised in the several projects for re-marriage entertained by her widower. During the period 1504-05 he considered marrying the young Queen of Naples, while at the same time he kept in mind the eligibility of the widowed Duchess of Savoy. Both tentative matches had political undertones; and it was for similar motives, after Ferdinand of Spain had allied with France (October, 1505) that Henry of England suddenly cast his thoughts in the direction of the lately widowed Juana, wife of the Duke of Burgundy and daughter of Ferdinand and Isabella. Her husband died in September, 1506, and by the following March Henry was already making overtures. Juana was in fact well advanced towards madness, and Henry's only motive in suggesting the match was to obtain control over Castile, with which Aragon had recently been in conflict. It is intriguing to consider that Catherine of Aragon, already singled out as a partner for the English Prince Arthur, was also the daughter of Ferdinand and Isabella. Even more singular is the circumstance that when Arthur died Henry seriously considered marrying Catherine himself.

The marriage of Henry VII and Elizabeth of York on January 18, 1486. This painting by the Flemish Jan van Mabuse shows the royal couple in an imaginary church which does not at all resemble Westminster Abbey, in which they were actually married.

18

War with France

The King our sovereign lord Henry, . . . doth you to understand that good, sure, and firm peace, union, and amity is made and concluded betwixt the King our said sovereign lord and the right high and mighty prince his cousin of France, their realms, countries, lordships, and subjects, during their life natural, and of either of them longer living, and by a year after the decease of him that last liveth; and that by this peace the subjects of the said realms, countries, and lordships, of what estate or condition they be, may haunt and be conversant by way of merchandise or otherwise, the one with the other, by land, by sea, and by rivers, without that they shall need safe-conduct, general or special; . . .

(Proclamation of Henry VII, December 12, 1492).

Strife with France had occupied the attentions of English monarchs for so long that it continued into Henry VII's reign almost inevitably, even though it was clear both to the king and his advisers that a usurper would do well to keep free of foreign involvement during the early years of his reign. On October 12, 1485 Henry announced a year's truce with France, and extended it to three years the following January; but Henry's hand was forced by matters beyond his control, his circumstances being complicated by numerous internal squabbles with which he had to contend, notably in the north of England.

A siege. From Holinshed's Chronicles.

The final impetus to England's beginning hostilities came, as so often in the past, because of an apparent ambitiousness on the part of France to increase its territorial interests in Europe: firstly in Brittany, but presumably later in Italy and then the Netherlands and finally Spain. Naturally Henry did not wish to witness England's traditional enemy increasing its influence in this manner; but although at the outset he tried to solve the problem by diplomatic means his efforts were crushed during May, 1488 when Edward Woodville, Lord Scales, Elizabeth of York's uncle, landed independently and against his monarch's wishes at St. Malo, in order to assist the Breton leaders. French and Breton troops, the latter with the support of Scales, met on July 28, 1488 at St. Aubin du Cormier, a number of the men of Brittany attired in English colours. Scales and his followers were almost completely routed. Henry at once offered profound apologies to the French king, Charles VIII, but his attempt to smooth the matter over was quickly dissipated when Duke Francis of Brittany died and left his daughter Anne under the guardianship of Marshal de Rieux, Francis having promised that his daughter should not form an alliance through marriage without the approval of the King of France. The annexation of Brittany, and with it the all important English entry to the Channel, became all at once a probability.

Once more Henry attempted mediation, proposing even that Anne should marry the English Duke of Buckingham. After the abandonment of this possible solution he employed his diplomacy in an attempt to stem the French advances in Brittany; but by early 1489 it had become clear that only military action would serve to correct the balance of power in western Europe. Obtaining funds from his subjects to finance such a venture proved more embarrassing to Henry than he had anticipated, being the cause of even further troubles in the north.

At the same time Henry wisely sought an alliance with Spain, whose King Ferdinand was in the process of rising to a position of considerable strength and whose sea power might prove especially valuable to any English cause. To cement friendly relations Henry proposed the marriage of a daughter of Spain and a son of England, and a treaty between the two powers was signed on March 27, 1489 (although it was never finally ratified). It was agreed that the young Catherine of Aragon was to be betrothed to Prince Arthur, but the date of her removal to London to accomplish this was not set.

In the meantime, although outwardly continuing to advance the cause of peace between England and France, Henry in fact was planning military action in Brittany. 6,000 English troops landed in Brittany in April, 1489 for the purpose of ousting the French, only to find their intentions thwarted as a result of internal disruption in Brittany and lack of support from the Dutch under their ruler Maximilian (King of the Romans). Anne of Brittany appeared resigned to the French annexation and Ferdinand of Spain offered no assistance at all to his new English ally. Henry thus had the option either of withdrawing, which would have allowed Charles a free hand in Italy if he wished it, or else of declaring full hostilities, thereby incurring the expense of arming and paying many more troops.

His circumstances improved through a series of new alignments that caused France to be virtually encircled by hostile powers. The English monarch signed a treaty with the Duke of Milan, who was concerned that Charles VIII might advance into his domain. When Maximilian announced his betrothal by proxy to the Duchess Anne of Brittany, Ferdinand of Spain despatched troops to Henry's assistance in the fear that Maximilian's authority in the Netherlands might become too pronounced and so the scene was set. Charles provided the final impetus: Anne of Brittany, now known as 'Queen of the Romans', gave up the long struggle to placate her own discontented troops, whom she could no longer afford to pay, and allowed the French king to march into her duchy and accepted the offer of his hand in marriage, in place of Maximilian's. The Pope granted a dispensation and the marriage took place on December 6, Brittany being then finally absorbed into France.

Spain meanwhile had been attacking Granada, which fell finally during January, 1492; while Maximilian had seen both his power and his prospects reduced intolerably. Although Henry could expect no firm assistance, therefore, the new French arrangements prompted him to act alone. Over the winter of 1491-92 the English parliament occupied itself with preparations for war. 500 ships were hired abroad, and Henry himself made ready to lead his troops into France. A fleet set forth during June, 1492, but returned quickly, Henry having delayed his expedition until the autumn.

Leaving Prince Arthur as his regent, the king was accompanied by 25,000 foot soldiers and 1,600 horse. He stayed a short while at Calais and then, on October 18, established a camp near Boulogne, his admiral Poynings having captured the port of Sluys on October 13. A siege lasting nine days was then begun, but in fact no truly ferocious fighting occurred and there were few casualties. Charles proposed a peace, and on November 3 it was signed at Etaples. Its provisions included a levy to Henry of some 750,000 gold crowns, 620,000 of them as payment against Henry's earlier expenditure in Brittany.

Henry's 'war' against France was thus resolved, and to many it appeared that he had simply undertaken a not too hazardous campaign against a traditional enemy solely to gratify his own martial instincts. He had hardly fought at all and had involved his backers in England with immense trouble and considerable expense. It was not a popular outcome, but it did provide Henry with the prospect of a period of peace that it was intended should endure until one year following the death of whichever of the signatories, Charles or himself, should be last to die. His son, Henry VIII, was in fact to honour this agreement almost to the letter.

Learning and the spread of printing

And for as moche as I suppose the said two bokes ben not had to fore this tyme in our English langage therefore I had the better will to accomplisshe this said werke whiche werke was begonne in Brugis and contynued in Gaunt, and finished in Coleyn, . . .

(Caxton's Prologue to his edition of Raoul le Fevre's *Recuyell of the Historye of Troye*, 1471).

Despite the violent manner in which he came to power and the various military exploits with which he concerned himself once on the throne, Henry VII established an era of comparative stability in England, at any rate on a social level. It is not surprising therefore that the arts should have flourished during his reign and that academic life should have been allowed its own freedom; but it was with the introduction of printing into England, and its development during Henry's reign, that the major cultural influence began to be felt.

It was in 1476 (or possibly early in 1477) that William Caxton had first begun printing in England. It was in 1485 that he published Sir Thomas Malory's famous *Morte D'Arthur*, a book whose tales of Arthurian chivalry in many ways reflected Henry's own attitude towards military exploits, though the book's medieval aspect perhaps also underlined the passing of that climate under the new Tudor regime in England, an era during which the facility for factual communications provided by the rise of printing effectively led England out of the so-called 'dark ages' into the Renaissance. In Italy this same Renaissance had come slightly earlier, heralded by a rebirth of classical studies, a renewed interest in the ancient Greek and Latin writings, their translations into the 'vulgar' Italian tongue and subsequent dissemination. In England the seeds of Italian example flowered only during Henry VIII's reign, but they were sown during that of his father.

Perhaps the most influential single factor in the development of learning and academicism was the decision on the part of Desiderius Erasmus to settle in England, at any rate for a trial period. He came to England first in 1499 and settled in Oxford. He was gracefully received by Henry VII, provided with lodgings in London by Sir Thomas More (whose residence was then on the banks of the Thames at Chelsea) and was in turn gratifyingly polite to the young 'Duke Henry', later Henry VIII, to whom he was introduced at Greenwich and for whom, in the space of three days, he wrote a poem entitled 'Prospopoeia Britanniae'. Over the ensuing decades Erasmus' connection with England flourished and his influence increased accordingly. He journeyed abroad on several occasions, but passed sufficient time in England for his name to appear in these pages at a later juncture.

William Caxton, father of English printing.

Henry VII's Chapel

AND we wol that our Towmbe bee in the myddes of the same Chapell, before the High Aultier, in such distance from the same, as it is ordred in the Plat made for the same Chapell, and signed with our hande: In which place we wol, that for the said Sepulture of us and our derest late wif the Quene, whose soule God p'donne, be made a Towmbe of Stone called Touche, sufficient in largieur for us booth.

(The Will of Henry VII).

overleaf:
The three children of Henry VII, c.1496. This remarkable triple portrait by Jan van Mabuse depicts three virtually unidentifiable children, nevertheless the probability is that they are intended for the children of Henry VII. Thus, from left to right, they are Arthur, Prince of Wales, Prince Henry and Margaret Tudor. Four copies exist in England of this painting now preserved at Sudeley Castle in Gloucestershire.

In 1503 Henry VII authorised the construction of a new chapel in West-minster Abbey to be named after himself. Here he was buried in 1509, although the chapel was not finally finished until several years later, requiring some twenty years all told to see completion. Henry VIII, once securely established on the English throne, sought to interfere with his father's plans for this chapel, but by and large it can be inspected today much as Henry VII projected it. Its particular merit lies in the fact that it shows to perfection the transition from the Perpendicular style of architecture, the final grandeur of the English Gothic, to the somewhat heavier Tudor style.

Henry VII's will, executed only a month before he died, set out his wishes for this chapel and the kind of funeral he wished to have in it. Among other items, the will provided for 10,000 masses to be said for Henry's soul; and in keeping with his usual parsimony he stipulated precisely how much should be paid for each (1,500 were to be said in honour of the Trinity, 2,500 in honour of the five wounds of Jesus Christ, 2,500 in honour of the joys of Our Lady, 450 in honour of the nine orders of angels, 150 in honour of the patriarchs, 600 in honour of the twelve apostles, and 2,300, 'which maketh up the hool nombre', in honour of all the saints). Henry also set aside funds for several charitable purposes, ensuring that, among other things, King's College at Cambridge should see completion. He also provided for £1,500 to be distributed among the poor, at a rate of 4d. for each person; a further £500 was set aside for the infirm residing in Westminster and the city of London and all debtors confined in prison for debts not exceeding £4.

The position of Henry VII's tomb in Westminster Abbey is close to those of both Henry V and Henry VI; beside him in effigy above the tomb is Elizabeth of York.

opposite:
Henry VII's Chapel at Westminster Abbey, with its fine Tudor vaulting and the large tomb of Henry and Elizabeth of York.

Henry VII's children

In all the devices and conceits of the triumphs of this marriage, there was a great deal of astronomy: the lady being resembled to Hesperus, and the Prince to Arcturus, and the old King Alphonsus, that was the greatest astronomer of Kings, and was ancestor to the lady, was brought in, to be the fortune-teller of the match. And whosoever had those toys in compiling, they were not altogether pedantical: but you may be sure, that King Arthur the Britain, and the descent of the Lady Catharine from the house of Lancaster, was in no wise forgotten. But, as it should seem, it is not good to fetch fortune from the stars: for the young Prince, that drew upon him at that time, not only the hopes and affections of his country, but the eyes and expectations of foreigners, after a few months, in the beginning of April, deceased at Ludlow Castle, . . .

(The marriage of Prince Arthur and Catherine of Aragon, from Francis Bacon's *History of the Reign of King Henry VII*, 1622).

Henry VII fathered five children, only four of whom survived infancy. The second, Henry, later became Henry VIII and is considered in his proper place in this book. The other children can be considered here according to their seniority.

Prince Arthur, who died the year before his mother in 1502, was born in Winchester on September 20, 1486. Presenting as he did tangible evidence of the union of the two houses of Lancaster and York, his birth was the cause of considerable rejoicing throughout the realm, whose citizens could look forward to a prolonged period of domestic peace. In 1489 he was created Prince of Wales and despatched by his father to live in the traditional Marcher property of Ludlow Castle. Here he was presumably amply cared for, and was only removed to London to meet his betrothed Catherine of Aragon, daughter of Ferdinand and Isabella of Spain.

Catherine landed at Plymouth on October 2, 1501; she journeyed to London slowly and arrived there on the 12th, the city being magnificently decorated in her honour. The couple were married two days later, Arthur being a year younger than the sixteen year old bride. The prince died of consumption the following year, leaving the young Princess of Wales both widowed and without any immediate prospects.

Before the time of his marriage Arthur had enjoyed every educational benefit appropriate for a future king. His classical studies, under the tutelage of the laureate Bernard André, were extensive. Homer, Virgil and Ovid were among the poets he read, Thucydides, Livy and Tacitus among the historians. Presumably, like his younger brother Henry, he would also have been thoroughly grounded in the rudiments of music, horsemanship and the skills of warfare. His premature death, although expected, was a tragic loss; the traveller Leland recorded that Arthur's parents were both greatly stricken at the news.

While Arthur was still alive, at the time of his marriage to Catherine, his sister Margaret was also the subject of public interest; for her betrothal to King James IV of Scotland had been announced and ambassadors from the northern kingdom were arriving in London to make final arrangements. As with the marriage of their own daughter to Arthur, Ferdinand and Isabella had been partly instrumental in bringing this match about.

Margaret Tudor was born on November 29, 1489, and was thus not quite twelve years old at the time of her betrothal to James of Scotland. The marriage was solemnised on August 8, 1502. From the point of view of subsequent events in the history of England this marriage is greatly intriguing, for one of the four children she bore James IV later became James V of Scotland, whose own daughter, Mary, Queen of Scots, gave birth in turn to James VI, who also became James I of England. However, widowed, Margaret also married Archibald, Earl of Angus, and their daughter Mary subsequently gave birth to that Henry, Lord Darnley, who married Mary, Queen of Scots. Thus two of Margaret Tudor's grandchildren, by separate marriages, were united to produce a future English monarch, though this time of the house of Stuart.

Margaret Tudor's life was one of continual upset. James IV was killed by Surrey's troops on Flodden Field on September 9, 1513. With him died his twenty year old son, then the Archbishop of St. Andrews and at one time a pupil of Erasmus. Margaret accordingly became regent, but she forfeited the position the following year when she married the Earl of Angus. This was not a satisfactory match and resulted in divorce in 1528. Her third marriage was to Henry, Lord Methuen, in whose home in Perthshire she died on October 4, 1541, her brother Henry VIII then occupying the English throne and her son James V that of Scotland. She was buried in the Carthusian monastery at Perth, her remains placed beside those of James I of Scotland.

Henry's fourth child, Mary Tudor, experienced similar though not so rigorous vicissitudes. She was born in 1497, and as early as December, 1507, in yet another of his diplomatic schemings, her father had succeeded in arranging

her betrothal to the Archduke Charles V of Castile, although by the time his manoeuvres were finally concluded the matter had ceased to be of primary importance to the wily English monarch and indeed was finally allowed to drop. It was resuscitated during the reign of Henry VIII following his defeat of the French at the 'Battle of Spurs' on August 16, 1513; then Mary was re-betrothed to Charles of Castile. Again the marriage did not take place, for in fact on August 7, 1514 a marriage contract was drawn up between Louis XII of France and Mary.

Mary was aghast at this proposal, but in an age when royal children of the feminine sex were regarded as no more than pawns in a game of intrigue and diplomacy she had no choice in the matter. She agreed only with reluctance, insisting upon the provision that when Louis died she should be allowed to choose her own second husband. In all probability she could look forward to this eventuality with a degree of optimism, for Louis was then 52 years of age, to her own seventeen years, and already he was considered an old man.

With the announcement of the forthcoming alliance through marriage it became possible to proclaim peace between England and France, on August 10, 1514. On August 18 a marriage by proxy took place in London and in October

opposite:
Mary Tudor, daughter of Henry VII and Elizabeth of York. This portrait was painted by Johannes Corvus and amply demonstrates why Mary was noted for her good looks and gentle disposition. The richly decorated under sleeve of her gown displays numerous embroidered Tudor roses.

31

the new Queen of France set sail to take up residence in her adopted country, her heart apparently set already on a prospective second husband, Charles Brandon, recently created Duke of Suffolk and already with matrimonial complications of his own.

Happily for Mary, Louis did not long survive his marriage and she was enabled to marry Suffolk secretly. In April, 1515 she and her new husband were allowed a public marriage at Greenwich in the presence of Henry VIII, who at first had expressed disapproval of her secret action but now welcomed the match. Mary had two children by her second marriage: Henry, Earl of Lincoln, and Frances, who became mother of Lady Jane Grey, by which link the latter unfortunate lady was proclaimed Queen of England and reigned without being crowned for only ten days before being imprisoned and subsequently beheaded. Mary died on January 23, 1534 at the age of 37. Her eminent husband survived her by eleven years, enjoying royal patronage throughout his life and being called upon to perform such miscellaneous duties as the suppression of the 'Pilgrimage of Grace' in 1536 and acting as one of the judges at the trial of Queen Catherine Howard.

James IV of Scotland and the Scottish question

The King our sovereign lord, Henry, by the grace of God King of England and of France and lord of Ireland, doth you to understand that, to the laud of God, the honour of our said sovereign lord, and the tranquility and great weal of his realm and subjects, there is taken, accorded, and concluded between his grace on the one party, and the right excellent, right high and mighty prince, his right dear and well-beloved brother and cousin James, King of Scots, on the other party, for them, their heirs and successors, realms, lands, countries, and places, whatsoever they be, their vassals, liegemen, and subjects, upon both sides, perpetual peace, firm and entire amity, league, and confederation, by land and by waters, to endure from the 24th day of January last past, forevermore and whilst the world shall endure, . . .

(Proclamation of Henry VII, Westminster, March 14, 1502).

James IV of Scotland reigned from 1488 until 1513 and spent a good deal of his time embroiled in hostilities with England, one of whose princesses he married but who did not succeed in containing his hostile instincts. As mentioned, he finally died in battle against English troops. He also became involved with the most notorious of all the pretenders who aspired to unseat Henry VII from his throne and who plagued the initial years of his reign.

When Perkin Warbeck, masquerading as the 'Duke of York', arrived in Stirling during November, 1495 to seek Scottish assistance in his 'cause' he was accorded a state welcome. James even arranged the marriage between

Warbeck and his own distant cousin, Lady Catherine Gordon. Warbeck, who claimed to be Richard of York, one of the two princes in the tower and by some mysterious process saved from supposed murder, and who enjoyed the mischievous support of certain of Henry VII's continental 'allies', met his death at Tyburn in 1499, but not before he had succeeded in causing a considerable amount of aggravation. At the instigation of Maximilian, King of the Romans, he had already made an expedition against England. He had not himself set foot on land, but something approaching 300 of his supporters had done so and all had perished. His visit to Scotland followed a disastrous offensive against Waterford in southern Ireland.

The Scotland he encountered existed quite independently of England. James IV had ascended the throne at the age of fifteen, quickly proving himself a mettlesome monarch, only his impetuousness acting against him and leading

Margaret Tudor, daughter of Henry VII, wife of James IV of Scotland and mother of James V.

eventually to his violent death. Scotland had long been an ally of France, the two countries united in their opposition to English interests. England was regarded as the aggressor, and thus during those periods when England and France were on amicable terms Scotland could look to France to be active on her behalf; when relations between England and France were poor the situation was reversed; moreover, France naturally held an interest in firing Scottish antagonism to English claims. Throughout the reigns of Henry VII and Henry VIII England and France were essentially at odds, and partly because of this, as well as the inevitable skirmishes that took place from either side of the English-Scottish border, the two British kingdoms were sometimes bitterly opposed. The marriage of Margaret Tudor to James IV was mooted as a pacific venture, but it served no lasting good in this respect. It was partly owing to the emergence of Warbeck that Henry VII was prompted to suggest this marriage; earlier he had offered the Scottish monarch his relative the Earl of Wiltshire's daughter, Catherine. A truce had been agreed between the two kingdoms in 1488, and when this expired in November, 1492 Henry secured its extension. Indeed, beyond doubt the English monarch's endeavours to secure good relations with Scotland were so pronounced there can be hardly any question but that subsequent hostilities were entirely of James' making.

Warbeck's appearance in Scotland, and his favourable reception, caused Henry little real dismay. Even on September 20, 1496, when Warbeck and a Scottish host crossed the border into England, Henry was unruffled: the northern English proved unwilling to join Warbeck, who promised them cash payment for their support. Scottish troops enjoyed themselves pillaging homesteads; then they recrossed the border the following day. Because the Scots had ignored the truce existing between the two nations Henry felt justified in seeking funds to meet future contingencies and to thwart the present; to his dismay he received rather less then half the £120,000 he had originally sought. In effect Henry used this ploy as a means of obtaining funds for his personal exchequer and he incurred a good deal of ill feeling in so doing, including a rebellion in Cornwall of people who asked why it was that miners should be taxed in order to pay for 'smal commocion made of ye Scottes'. Further similar rebellions erupted elsewhere.

In July, 1497 Henry asked James to surrender Warbeck and to re-establish the truce conditions that had existed between the two kingdoms before the arrival of the pretender. Spain attempted at this time to gain influence in Scotland, suggesting a marriage between James and one of Ferdinand's daughters (though in point of fact Ferdinand did not then have eligible offspring to hand). To placate Henry, the Scottish monarch summarily dismissed Warbeck; and to please Ferdinand he made it plain that the hostilities with England would continue. Warbeck sailed away under surveillance, but as soon as he could made for Cornwall where he hoped to gain impetus from the current unrest. He advanced into Devon, amassing a sizeable following, but before long his strength was exhausted and he was captured at Beaulieu after fleeing.

The Scots attacked once more, towards the end of July, 1497. Surrey successfully counter-attacked. James himself led his men, and even went so far as to suggest deciding the outcome by single combat between himself and Surrey. The result of this particular 'adventure' was the signing of yet another peace treaty between England and Scotland at Ayton, on September 30, 1497, which endured for seven almost harmonious years. The two kingdoms continued in alliance throughout the remainder of Henry's reign, the only recorded skirmishes occurring along the border, between borderers.

There were certain moments of concern when Duke Charles of Gelders, an ally of Louis of France, asked the Scottish monarch for aid against Philip of Burgundy. Both James and Henry were allied with Philip, but James was

Charles' kinsman and he could do nothing other than warn Henry that if Burgundy continued with her offensive, and England assisted her, he would feel bound to come to Charles' assistance. In fact however the risk of hostilities was slight, and James well knew this.

Trade and travel under Henry VII

And if any packer presume to pack any wools contrary to the form of this present ordinance, that then he be put from his office of packing, and to be punished for his perjury at the King's pleasure; and if the said wool be wrong packed by the fraud and knowledge or consent of the merchant buyer thereof, contrary to the tenor of this ordinance, and thereupon the same merchant to be thereof convicted before the treasurer of England for the time being, by good, true, and indifferent men, that then the merchant or merchants so convicted shall forfeit for every sack so fraudulently packed, as often as he or they shall so offend, £20 sterling, whereof the King's highness shall have £15, and £5 shall be paid to him that detecteth the said false packing; . . .

(Proclamation of Henry VII, announcing Trade Treaty with Burgundy, Westminster, May 18, 1499).

A glance at the chronology included towards the end of this publication will serve to illustrate that Henry's reign was not devoted entirely to foreign wars and domestic restraint; a significant advance in mercantilism can also be detected. During the reigns of his two illustrious successors, Henry VIII and Elizabeth I, England's trading activities were boosted vastly; during Henry VII's reign important preparatory steps were taken. The golden age of discovery that was to flower during the time of Elizabeth, resulting in international trading on an unprecedented level, knew its first encouragement during Henry VII's reign. European trading had of course flourished for many years.

Henry was fully aware of the importance of commerce generally for the enrichment of the nation as a whole, and did all in his power to facilitate it. One of his earliest actions, when firmly established on the throne, was to enter into a commercial treaty with Denmark, in January, 1490, which had the effect of establishing English interests in an area directly affecting traders of the Hanseatic League (a number of Hanse towns organised into a trading league and originating in the thirteenth century, whose privileges in England and elsewhere had long been a bone of contention with English merchants). Over the ensuing decade this new arrangement was much consolidated, although in 1504 the English parliament passed an act guaranteeing Hanseatic privileges in England. During the same period Henry also succeeded in improving trading arrangements with both the Venetians and the Florentines. English wool and cloth provided primary export materials at this time, and in return England imported spices, wines, glassware and a significant number of printed books.

Mercantile endeavours on a European level, during the same period it must be remembered when Christopher Columbus was in the process of sailing to

Sebastian Cabot, son of the great John Cabot. The younger Cabot was one of the large number of fifteenth and early sixteenth century mariners who believed in the existence of a 'North-West Passage'.

America (1492), can conveniently be said to have begun on England's part about the year 1490, when John Cabot came to England. In 1496 he obtained a patent of privileges to make a voyage of discovery, having been granted the previous year the right, together with his three sons, their heirs and deputies, to sail under the English flag throughout the world. The Cabots were to meet all their own expenses and allocate 20% of their profits to the king. They were to be allowed sole trading rights in any territories discovered by them and enjoyed certain excise benefits.

Since it was now known that the world was round, it was generally held that by sailing west from Europe one must inevitably strike the eastern coastline of the Asiatic continent, whose spices were otherwise obtainable only through the agencies of Venetian traders and others. Untold wealth was expected to accrue from the discovery of this continent, and it was assumed that the sea voyage would be a relatively short one. When on June 24, 1497, after a voyage of almost two months duration, Cabot put in to land at what was probably either Newfoundland or Nova Scotia, he quite naturally assumed that he had discovered the Asian continent and that if he followed the coastline south he would strike the rich lands he knew of from the tales of eastern venturers.

Cabot made a second voyage in 1498, but he and his boats never returned. Interest had however been inspired, and further expeditions were undertaken, the Portuguese entering into active competition with the English. In March, 1501, Henry issued letters patent similar to those granted earlier to Cabot, to six men, three of whom were English and three Portuguese, and in this year a joint Anglo-Portuguese expedition to North America was undertaken. Other voyages followed, leading to a quick realisation that the golden shores of Cathay had not in fact been struck; but Henry continued to grant his ready patronage to all adventurers who sailed to the new land, eager for the discovery of a widely anticipated 'North-West Passage' which it was assumed would make the voyage to the east an easy one. No such passage existed, and many were the mariners who over the years perished in quest of it.

John Cabot's son Sebastian was one of those who believed the passage existed. With the aid of royal backing he set sail at some date subsequent to 1505 and penetrated what was probably Hudson Bay, which he hailed as the passage itself. Ice prevented his further progress at that time and he therefore explored the North American coastline for additional openings, travelling almost as far south as what is today Delaware Bay. Still he sought in vain, but remained confident of ultimate success. He returned to England only to discover that Henry VII was dead and the throne occupied by a monarch far more intrigued by European matters and concrete trading results than the dreams of world travellers.

The spate of maritime enterprises naturally awakened the interests of merchants, notably in the ports of the south and west of England, such as Bristol, a city which through this activity was destined to become immensely prosperous. It was here, in 1506, that the 'Company Adventurers into the New Found Lands' was organised. In any consideration of the reign of Henry VII, a reign during which political power and economic success were both prominent factors, the two connected pursuits of trading and discovery must play a major part. Both were to develop extensively throughout the Tudor era.

Part Two

Henry VIII

The young Prince Henry

The king was young and lusty, disposed all to mirth and pleasure, and to follow his desire and appetite, nothing minding to travail in the busy affairs of this realm. The which the almoner perceived very well, and took upon him therefore to disburden the king of so weighty a charge and troublesome business that should necessarily happen in the council, as long as he, being there and having the king's authority and commandment, doubted not to see all things sufficiently furnished and perfected; . . . And whereas the other ancient counsellors would, according to the office of good counsellors, divers times persuade the king to have sometime an intercourse in to the council, there to hear what was done in weighty matters, the which pleased the king nothing at all, for he loved nothing worse than to be constrained to do any thing contrary to his royal will and pleasure; . . .

(George Cavendish: *The Life of Cardinal Wolsey*).

Henry VIII was not yet eighteen years of age when he came to the throne; he was ten at the time of his brother Arthur's death when he was suddenly upgraded from a humble Duke of York, apparently intended for the Church and the see of Canterbury, to become heir to the English throne. The progress of his earlier upbringing was therefore rudely interrupted and of necessity changed to fit him for his future kingly duties.

Tilting. An illustration from Holinshed's Chronicles.

Henry was born on June 28, 1491 at Greenwich Palace. On October 31, 1494 he was declared Duke of York and two months later he was made warden of the Scottish Marches. Other offices and honours accompanied and succeeded these, but by and large they were of a purely nominal character. For the first decade of his life Henry's status and education were considered secondary in importance to those of his elder brother Arthur, and to some extent it is clear that the prince was a neglected, even lonely youngster.

His education was not however completely neglected, and it appears that by the early age of five years he had already been placed under the tutelage of the poet laureate, John Skelton, who in 1501 wrote a 'Speculum Principis' for his pupil, a handbook to princely conduct. Presumably Henry also underwent some of the classical instruction that had been the lot of his brother. Following his accession first of all to the Dukedom of Cornwall and then to the Princedom of Wales, the latter on February 18, 1503, it appears that his life became severely restricted, his father neither jeopardising his health by posting him to such a station as Ludlow, which had resulted in his brother's death, nor allowing him any apprenticeship or even instruction in the art of government. His companions were selected for him and his comings and goings strictly limited. From an early age he had been instructed in foreign language and in the art of music, and all his life he was to practise these skills, but by and large his childhood was an unsatisfactory one for a future monarch, one whom his father doubtless envisaged as eventually occupying the strongest throne in Europe.

Henry's favourite sport, at which he was highly proficient, was tilting. Throughout his young manhood he was to pursue this interest, as well as other open-air sports, particularly falconry. In all likelihood the brashness accompanying the earlier years of his reign, and the seeming flamboyance of this 'Renaissance Prince', can be seen as a direct reaction to a somewhat stultified adolescence. Henry's occasional thoughtlessness as king doubtless sprang from his lack of political instruction and hence experience.

One other curious factor is attached to Henry's childhood. In an age when marriages were arranged between ruling houses simply through diplomatic considerations, often at ludicrously early ages (even if in certain instances parents did not really intend the marriages to take place), it is strange that the young prince should never have been affianced to anybody; for until the age of ten he was not the heir apparent and could well have been bespoken for some continental princess in the interests of bringing about an alliance. That this did not occur can perhaps be ascribed to Henry's VII's feeling that an English prince should not be bargained away for a foreign princess, even though an English princess might be married off to whoever seemed most convenient at the time. Once he came to the throne Henry's predicament was temporarily solved by his marrying his brother Arthur's widow, Catherine of Aragon.

Physically, the young Henry was completely different from the later portrayals of the monarch. Even in early manhood he was slim. Surviving suits of armour from his early and later life betray notable differences in girth, while one portrait of Henry as a young man shows him reasonably narrow in the face, though immediately identifiable by his firm jaw and pouting lower lip. The eyes, as throughout his life, mingle shrewdness and slyness. It is difficult to set the young Henry alongside the mature monarch; equally well, it is not easy to accept that the athletic young man was to develop into possibly the greatest king England has ever known.

opposite:

The embarkation of Henry VIII for the 'Field of Cloth of Gold', by an unknown artist. The meeting which took place between Francis I of France and Henry VIII of England in 1520 provided an opportunity for the two men to come face to face for the first time. Henry's departure, together with a large retinue, took place from Dover on May 31. In this painting Dover Castle can be seen in the background, while various parties are boarding their ships in the foreground. Henry's flagship, Harry Grace a Dieu, *can be seen in the centre foreground, the royal coat of arms emblazoning its stern. Altogether about 5,000 English men and women were transported to Calais in order to participate in this event.*

Henry VIII and France

Also that after the watch shall be set, unto the time it be relieved in the morning, no manner of man make no shouting, blowing of horns, nor none other whistling or great noise, but if it be trumpets by a special commandment, upon pain of imprisonment and further to be punished at the discretion of the marshal. . . .

Also that every horseman at the first blast of the trumpet do saddle his horse, at the second to bridle, at the third to leap on his horse's back to wait on the King or his lord or captain. And that every man wait unto the standard of his own lord and captain, and not to depart therefrom, nor to meddle with none other companies in riding nor going, but such as be commanded, as harboragers and other carriers, . . . Upon pain of imprisonment . . .

(Proclamation of Henry VIII, concerning English troops in France, London, May, 1513).

Henry ascended the English throne on April 22, 1509, his coronation taking place on June 24 of that year. Two weeks before the latter event he was married to Catherine of Aragon. Once enthroned, Henry immediately set about justifying his kingship, and before many years had elapsed he was considering a new English campaign in France. He did not actually accompany his own troops at the outset, but he made his influence felt among the French.

An Anglo-French treaty was in fact signed in March of 1510 (though two months later Henry signed a separate treaty with Spain which had the effect of reducing the French treaty in significance), but even so from the outset of his reign Henry harboured antagonistic feelings against the French. It seemed that all he required was a satisfactory ally with whom he could jointly campaign against England's traditional foe. Henry's early policy was equally irresponsible with regard to Scotland, and as will be seen in the appropriate place he found himself bitterly opposed to the Scottish kingdom.

The course of his hostilities with France was frequently directed by the influence of Ferdinand of Spain, who was as wily as Henry's own father had been and as Henry demonstrably was not as yet. Ferdinand possessed the additional advantage over the young Tudor sovereign of being Henry's father-in-law.

Henry's opportunity came fortuitously, at the instigation of Pope Julius II, who during 1511 was himself riding at the head of Papal troops, supported by armies from Switzerland and Spain, in an attempt to expel invading French troops from different parts of Italy. Julius approached Henry for assistance, and Ferdinand advised the English monarch to acquiesce, himself hoping to procure the territory of Navarre as reward for his own help. Henry's ministers opposed the scheme; nor did he have the excuse that France was being delinquent in meeting her financial commitments in the form of pensions resulting from her treaty with England. However, in 1511 Henry despatched two small expeditionary forces to support first of all Margaret of the Netherlands against the Duke of Gelders and secondly Ferdinand against the Moors, the latter of which returned, unrequired, without contributing anything beyond riotous behaviour at Cadiz.

These were but footholds on the continent: on October 4, 1511 the Vatican and Venice, joined by Spain, formed a Holy League to defend the papacy against its enemies; on November 13 Henry also acceded to this league, and within six months had agreed with Ferdinand to launch an attack upon France. During April, 1512 Henry's army prepared to put to sea and in June a host of some 10,000 landed near Fuenterrabia at the behest of Ferdinand (who duly took advantage of its presence to mask his own activities while he overran Navarre). Intelligence had already been received that the papal forces had suffered a severe setback, and this provided Henry with his final spur to action; but before his troops could move to the Pope's aid they ran short of food and beer (the latter an essential beverage in an age when water could not be relied upon for drinking purposes), many of them contracted dysentry, several died, and in October they deserted, making their own way home. The only notable outcome of the expedition was a series of victories at sea and along the French coast engineered by the English admiral, Sir Edward Howard. In revenge Louis tried to persuade James IV of Scotland to attack England.

Peace came to Europe for a time, Ferdinand boasting the territorial gains he had anticipated and hoping for more. The Pope, and in his wake the young Henry VIII anxious to restore some of his lost dignity, made plans to revive the struggle. On April 5, 1513 Julius and Henry formed a treaty, together with Ferdinand and Maximilian, King of the Romans, to declare war on France yet again. On April 20 the English fleet set sail for Brest, was duly trounced by the French at sea and returned to Plymouth on April 30. Thomas Howard then succeeded his brother as admiral and the English force continued with its

Deal Castle. Henry VIII was the last of the English castle builders with purely defensive aims in mind. He built numerous such structures along the southern coast of England, smaller castles than those built by his predecessors and intended exclusively to prevent French troops from landing. In addition to Deal he built castles at Cowes, Camber, Southsea, Walmer, Sandgate, Sandown, Queenborough and elsewhere. Henry was not however blind to the fact that English defences must be concentrated on her sea power, and it had been with this factor uppermost in his mind that he had caused the Royal Dockyard at Woolwich to be founded.

Henry VIII. An old woodcut.

preparations. By the end of May 14,000 English troops disembarked at Calais under the Earl of Shrewsbury and Sir Charles Somerset (Lord Herbert). On June 1 a further 11,000 men arrived under Henry in person, joining the first troops near the town of Thérouanne. Together with Maximilian's army, on August 16, 1513 the French army attempting to relieve Thérouanne was beaten at Guinegatte, in an action better known as the 'Battle of Spurs'.

Thérouanne was captured on August 23; Tournai was besieged a week or so later and it too was captured on September 21. Persuaded that his martial honour had been satisfied, the young English king returned home, a conqueror, on October 21. Thus this latest round in the prolonged enmity was credited to the English side, together with its allies. Other campaigns were to follow, though not for several years.

The various European powers continued with their policy of forming alliances and cross-alliances, and then conveniently forgetting that they had entered into any theoretically binding agreements whatsoever. For a while England remained aloof, partly because for the time being Henry was satisfied with the victorious outcome of the 'Spurs' campaign and partly because his damaged finances would not allow him to incur any foreign commitments for some time. In furtherance of this latest policy, Thomas Wolsey, who had emerged as Henry's chief minister, was ever active in the field of continental intrigue. On April 30, 1527 a concluding treaty — the Peace of Amiens — was signed between England and France, having been negotiated entirely at Wolsey's instigation. In the meantime, during 1526, Henry had been appointed protector of a new confederation of states known as the League of Cognac, consisting of England, the Vatican, France, Florence, Venice and Milan, all dedicated to frustrating the Italian designs of Charles V, King of Castile.

The peace with France was temporary and uneasy: on January 21, 1528 England once again declared war on France. The powerful Wolsey, who held virtually unopposed sway in English affairs by this time, was behind this latest enterprise, just as earlier he had been principally instrumental in preserving the peace. Unfortunately for Wolsey he did not have the full support of his countrymen and could not muster an army. His failure in this instance was to lead to his downfall.

Wolsey and others

Perceiving a plain path to walk in towards promotion, he handled himself so politicly, that he found the means to be one of the king's council, and to grow in good estimation and favour with the king, to whom the king gave a house at Bridewell, in Fleet Street, sometime Sir Richard Empson's, where he kept house for his family, and he daily attended upon the king in the court, being in his especial grace and favour, having then great suit made unto him, as counsellors most commonly have that be in favour. His sentences and witty persuasions in the council chamber were always so pithy that they always, as occasion moved them, assigned him, for his filed tongue and ornate eloquence, to be their expositor unto the king's majesty in all their proceedings. In whom the king conceived such a loving fantasy, especially for that he was most earnest and readiest among all the council to advance the king's only will and pleasure, without any respect to the case. The king, therefore, perceived him to be a meet instrument for the accomplishment of his devised will and pleasure, called him more near unto him, and esteemed him so highly that his estimation and favour put all other ancient counsellors out of their accustomed favour, that they were in before; insomuch that the king committed all his will and pleasure unto his disposition and order. . . .

(George Cavendish: *The Life of Cardinal Wolsey*).

Thomas Wolsey was Henry VIII's first powerful minister, one moreover with a massive seniority in the Church and latterly with designs on the papal throne itself. He was born in 1471, educated at Magdalen College, Oxford and graduated at the age of fifteen. He began his professional life in diplomatic circles and because of his success in this departure was appointed first of all to be Dean of Lincoln Cathedral. When Henry VIII came to the throne Wolsey at once ingratiated himself with the youthful monarch; he was raised to the Bishopric of Lincoln and then, in 1514, Archbishopric of York. He succeeded Archbishop Warham as Chancellor the following year; at the same time he was raised by Pope Leo X to the College of Cardinals. From then until the time of his downfall in 1529 Wolsey was the most powerful man in England and one of the most influential of all European ministers.

His achievements were remarkable. He combined ecclesiastical authority with that of the state, and until the time of Henry's divorce from Catherine of Aragon rarely allowed them to conflict. But although Wolsey appeared to wield supreme power, even to the extent of acting without consulting his sovereign,

CARDINAL WOOLSEY

as Henry VIII matured in his regality he began to exercise an ever more emphatic restraint over his underlings, never allowing matters to fall completely beyond his control.

Wolsey possessed unbounded ambition and a very real greatness. His love of power was perhaps paramount in his make-up, but the continued acquisition of preferments carried with it an increase in fortune on a lavish scale and this too was an important trait of Wolsey. His promotion to the rank of cardinal was an example of the first of these two sides of his greed, a papal appointee of this rank being held the senior even of a country's most influential ministers, certainly of her archbishops and bishops. He consolidated the appointment by persuading the Pope to appoint him also the papal legate *a latere*, a situation

William Warham as Archbishop of Canterbury.

Title page of the complete works of Sir Thomas More published in 1557, twenty two years after his death.

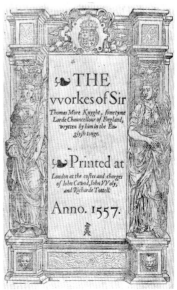

opposite:

Hampton Court Palace, built by Wolsey in 1515, was presented to the king in 1525. Wolsey's plans for this palace, although they did not prove wholly satisfying in execution, nevertheless provided a model for future palaces in England, including the concept of two courtyards, an outer and an inner. The typical Tudor tower gatehouse was also incorporated in this structure, and over this was placed the famous astronomical clock shown here. It indicates not only the time of day but also the configurations of the sun and moon. Its maker was Nicholas Oursian.

transforming him into the Pope's actual representative in England, with full papal authority at his own command. His king being in theory the ecclesiastical subject of the Vicar-General in Rome, and Wolsey that dignitary's local deputy, it was evident that conflict could easily flare up between monarch and legate. That Henry did not allow this to occur for several years, appreciating as he did his minister's indomitable and wilful cunning, was a remarkable achievement. Wolsey attempted to have this extreme papal favour bestowed upon him for life, but it was not until later that Pope Clement VII finally conceded the point.

Wolsey's authority in England was exceptionally strong. William Warham, Archbishop of Canterbury, was forced to acknowledge the cardinal his superior; indeed, the archbishop's own clergy looked to Wolsey for guidance rather than to Warham. Even more forceful was his attitude towards parliament, which he

caused to be dissolved, its members meeting only once over the fourteen year period preceding his downfall. He caused Sheffield, Speaker of the House, to be imprisoned in the Tower at the time of the dissolution, where the unfortunate parliamentarian at last expired; and when in 1523 parliament finally reconvened temporarily, in order to vote much needed funds, even then Wolsey contrived matters so that the house's vote was no more than a formality. Rarely can one man have enjoyed such absolute deployment of national resources; but, as has been often pointed out, although Wolsey did not abuse power — seeking it merely for its own sake — neither did he employ it for the national good. He used it basically for intrigue and self-aggrandisement. As far as the benefices of organised religion were concerned, for example, Wolsey took for himself virtually everything that he required, and he personally held several archbishoprics and bishoprics in England.

This then was Wolsey, whose influence was felt on almost all levels. He fell abruptly, as was almost inevitable. Ultimately it was his manipulation of papal affairs, and particularly Henry's need to divorce Catherine of Aragon, that caused his unseating, or at any rate gave it the spur.

Basically, by 1529 his influence was on the wane, his wishes were not always being humoured. Revenge, or at any rate the pleasure of watching the mighty tumble, prompted clerics and statesmen alike to countenance, and then engineer, the cardinal's downfall. His failure to raise an army against France was one contributory factor; his unwillingness to pursue the question of Henry's divorce from Catherine far stronger. Henry himself was the final arbiter of Wolsey's downfall, simply by ignoring his subordinate's pleas to be heard. The cardinal was finally exiled to his archbishopric in York (where he was able to maintain the splendour of his way of life, and from where he attempted vainly to revitalise his diminished authority), the first time he had visited this see since his appointment to it. He returned to London, and there, undoubtedly, the ultimate disgrace which he had so far eluded — imprisonment in the Tower and execution — would have awaited him. Happily for himself Wolsey died of natural causes, on November 24, 1530, the Tower guard already in attendance.

His successor was Sir Thomas More, but he never enjoyed the might which had been Wolsey's: Henry had learnt his lesson. More was born in 1478, and like his predecessor in the office of Lord Chancellor had studied at Oxford. An intellectual before all else, he had there made the acquaintance of Erasmus. So far as posterity is concerned, his greatest achievement was the authorship of the seminal *Utopia*. As a statesman and diplomat however he cut no mean figure in his day and amassed a large fortune. He was elected a Privy Councillor in 1516, knighted in 1522 and appointed Speaker of the House of Commons the following year. Like Wolsey, he did not approve of Henry's divorcing Catherine of Aragon, and eventually this cost him not only his office but his life, having refused to acquiesce to the Act of Supremacy. He lost his head on Tower Hill on May 6, 1535. His last words as he settled his head tranquilly on the block, and brushed aside his beard so that it should not be cut were: 'Pity that should be cut, that has not committed treason'.

Wolsey and More were the two principal statesmen of the first half of Henry VIII' reign. The latter half was to be dominated by Thomas Cromwell. There were of course numerous other prominent men surrounding the king at this time. Archbishop William Warham, although obliged to assume a subservient role to the autocratic Wolsey, held the see of Canterbury from 1503 to 1532, not surviving his arch opponent by very long. Before Wolsey's coming he had also occupied the high office of Lord Chancellor. To his credit, Warham did not accept Wolsey's show of power without returning a degree of coldness, never signing off his letters to the latter with any more flattering style than 'At your grace's commandment'. The Great Seal he had surrendered at Wolsey's

opposite:

Thomas More by Holbein, probably one of the finest examples of portraiture dating from Henry VIII's reign. More is depicted wearing his black, fur-trimmed gown and a Tudor rose pendant. Shown here in his prime, the Lord Chancellor is without the beard he grew in later life.

A Henry VIII sovereign of 1543. The third issue of this denomination in Henry's reign, this coin is of interest for the inclusion of the title 'King of Ireland'. The obverse side, with the king seated in majesty, is shown here.

opposite:
*Catherine of Aragon, painted in
middle age by an unknown artist.*

promotion was offered to him again at the cardinal's fall, but he refused it on account of his advanced age.

Warham was succeeded as Archbishop of Canterbury by Thomas Cranmer, himself destined to burn at the stake but in his day an extremely powerful personage. He it was who finally annulled Henry's marriage to Catherine of Aragon and declared valid his secret marriage to Anne Boleyn. He was born in 1489, educated at Cambridge, and is perhaps best remembered for having obtained Henry's permission for copies of the new translation of the Bible to be placed in every church in the kingdom for public reading. Throughout Henry's reign he enjoyed patronage, attending the monarch in his dying moments. He crowned the 'boy king', Edward VI, but at the accession of Mary I he was committed to the Tower, at the same time as Ridley and Latimer. In an endeavour to save his life he recanted, but realising that his enemies were determined to put him to death in any case he withdrew his recantation. He was burnt at the stake on March 21, 1556, making the famous gesture before he died of thrusting his hand pointedly into the flames and declaring that the hand which had sinned in writing a recantation should be the first part of his body to suffer. His heresy had been to play a part in the establishment of an English Church. During 1554 England was reconciled with Rome, and Roman Catholicism was restored. The marriage of priests was once again frowned upon, and Cranmer, among his other 'heresies', had twice married and fathered several children.

A few other key figures of Henry's reign may be briefly mentioned. Sir Thomas Audley, created Baron Audley in 1538, was Lord Chancellor from 1533 to 1544; he was succeeded by Thomas, Lord Wriothesley, who held the office until 1548 during Edward VI's reign. John Russell, created Earl of Bedford in 1550, was Keeper of the Privy Seal from 1542 until his death in 1555. The two Thomas Howards, father and son and successive Dukes of Norfolk, held the important office of Treasurer, the first from 1501 until 1522, the second until the end of Henry's reign, being appointed Earl Marshal in 1533. All these men played important roles in the government of Henry VIII's England, many of them contributing to some of the more unsavoury events of their master's lifetime. Baron Audley, for instance, presided at the trial of Sir Thomas More, whose office he had inherited. Thomas Howard the younger, the third Duke of Norfolk, contributed to the articles compiled against Wolsey, leading to the latter's fall. His own fall came in 1546, when Henry accused him of trying to deprive him of the crown; at his trial he was found guilty and sentenced to be beheaded. By good fortune, as far as Norfolk was concerned, the king died before this could be put into effect, and although he remained in the Tower throughout Edward VI's reign he was freed at the accession of Mary and restored to his former dignity, dying in 1554.

The six wives of Henry VIII

Forasmuch as the unlawful matrimony between the King's highness and the Lady Catherine, Princess Dowager, late wife to Prince Arthur, by just ways and means is lawfully dissolved, and a divorce and separation had and done between his said highness and the said Lady Catherine, by the most reverend father in God the Archbishop of Canterbury, Legate and Primate of all England, and Metropolitan of the same; and thereupon the King's majesty hath lawfully married and taken to his wife, after the laws of the church, the right high and excellent Princess Lady Anne, now Queen of England, . . .

And yet nevertheless the King's most gracious pleasure is that the said Lady Catherine shall be well used, obeyed, and entreated according to her honor and noble parentage, by the name, title, state, and style of Princess Dowager, as well by all her officers, servants, and ministers as also by others his humble and loving subjects, in all her lawful business and affairs, so it extend not in anywise contrary to this proclamation.

(Proclamation of Henry VIII, London, July 5, 1533).

A great measure of both personal and more widespread tragedy is attached to the history of Henry VIII and his wives. The wives themselves are normally and rightly taken to have been victims of circumstance; yet Henry's own predicament was by no means negligible, and the troubles he created for himself and his ministers provided continual aggravation. Two lives were sacrificed in the quest to secure Henry a male heir; England was severed from Rome; and as is so often the case in matters of government, personal problems often interrupted the administration of the realm.

Catherine of Aragon was the first of Henry's wives, betrothed to him while he was still a boy of twelve and she the widow of his elder brother, Prince Arthur. Her premature bereavement had proved particularly unpleasant for the princess, for lack of funds had severely restricted her activities, and as long as she remained in England she was virtually confined to Durham House, in the Strand. Henry VII had decided on his son's marriage to Catherine immediately following Arthur's death, the provision being that the young prince should marry his princess as soon as he attained the age of fifteen. Because of Catherine's widowed circumstances it was necessary to obtain a papal dispensation, but although a formal betrothal took place the marriage was not solemnised until after Henry VIII's succession.

This first marriage lasted many years, and it was not until 1533 that Henry divorced Catherine. Unlike two of her successors, Henry's first wife did not perish on the scaffold; she was dismissed and retired first of all to Ampthill in Bedfordshire, then later to Kimbolton Castle in Huntingdonshire, dying on January 7, 1536. Of the seven children she bore Henry (including four sons)

The handwriting of Catherine of Aragon in 1513.

only the future Queen Mary survived. When Henry decided to divorce Catherine he precipitated a papal crisis that was to lead first of all to his own excommunication, then to the severance of the English Church from that of Rome and indirectly to the dissolution of the monasteries. Henry's parting from Catherine, when it came, was not a sudden occurrence but had been broached over a period of years, the queen herself resolutely opposing the idea.

Wolsey was instrumental in Catherine's dismissal, but not responsible for it. He was not pleased at the prospect of Henry marrying Anne Boleyn, and had in mind instead a French bride; he consoled himself with the reflection that Henry would probably discard Anne after a while in any case. It was in 1524 that Henry seriously began to contemplate divorce. His only living male offspring was an illegitimate son by Elizabeth Blount, and in 1525 he created this young man Duke of Richmond and Somerset as well as appointing him Lord High

opposite:
Henry VIII's writing desk.

61

Admiral, Warden of the Marches and Lord Lieutenant of Ireland; but Henry cannot really have believed that in the event of there being no other male heir this son would be allowed to succeed to the throne, and because of this he knew he must produce a legitimate male heir. Wolsey was ordered to have the marriage with Catherine declared null, basing his deliberations on his recent declaration that the deaths of the queen's children had come about through divine intervention, just deserts for what he considered an incestuous marriage, and therefore by definition invalid. As papal representative in England Wolsey was of course empowed to undertake many businesses, but in the matter of declaring null a marriage which had only been arranged through papal dispensation he was powerless.

The situation which arose when Wolsey sought to have the issue decided at the court of Rome was so tricky, so influenced by diplomatic considerations, that neither the Pope nor Wolsey himself felt able to move definitively, and the question of Henry's separation from Catherine lingered. Catherine herself asserted that since her union with Arthur had never been consummated her marriage to Henry was not in any way incestuous. For his drawn-out diplomacy and his unwillingness to offend either Pope or king Wolsey was removed from office, the problem of Catherine still unresolved, though as far as Henry was concerned she had been effectively dismissed.

Anne Boleyn, who had been a lady in waiting to Catherine for some time, had long held the king's attention (and it is affirmed that both her sister and her mother had already consorted with the monarch). That Anne determinedly repulsed his advances only had the effect of firing Henry's desire for her, and on November 14, 1532, without waiting for papal approval, Henry and Anne were married. On Whit Sunday, 1533 she was publicly crowned in Westminster Abbey and on September 7 of that year gave birth to the Princess Elizabeth, destined to be the last Tudor monarch.

Anne, created Countess of Pembroke in her own right in 1533, was not to benefit long from her new ascendancy. A woman of good looks, educated and a one-time resident at the court of France, she had acquired both refinement and a familiarity with easy morals. She may have refused to succumb to Henry's advances for a long time before her marriage to him, but once married she did not spurn the advances of many others, including it was said her own brother, Viscount Rochfort. If she failed to produce the required male heir her fate would easily be determined.

On January 29, 1536, following Henry's excommunication and the initiation of his policy of dissolving the English religious houses, Anne suffered a miscarriage, and having rid himself of one mate Henry determined to rid himself of this one also. He ordered certain of his advisers to look into the question of treason in all its aspects, seeking by this method to indict and then incriminate his wife. Adultery appeared the most easily established pretence, and this therefore was duly proclaimed as Anne's offence. On May 15, 1536 she appeared before a tribunal headed by her uncle, the Duke of Norfolk; she was found guilty and on May 19 she was beheaded. Her executioner had been brought specially from Calais, being held particularly adept at his profession and, so it was said, sent for by Henry in anticipation several days before Anne's guilt was actually established.

Anne was succeeded by Jane Seymour, eldest daughter of Sir John Seymour of Wolf Hall in Wiltshire. Born in 1509, the year of her future husband's accession, Jane had been a lady in waiting to Anne Boleyn. Like her predecessor she had soon attracted the king's eye, and with quite indecent haste she married Henry on May 20, 1536, only twenty four hours after her old mistress' decapitation. Unlike her two predecessors she produced the desired male heir, the future Edward VI. Twelve days afterwards, on October 24, 1537, she died at Hampton Court.

opposite:
Anne of Cleves, a portrait now in the possession of St. John's College, Oxford. This lovely example of sixteenth century portraiture amply demonstrates how Henry VIII could have been attracted to his fifth wife through the medium of another portrait.

Surrounding the circumstances of Henry's marriage to Jane were all manner of vexations. Although the king could doubtless have achieved the match without undue formality, it was felt desirable for Cranmer to go through the motions of declaring that the marriage to Anne Boleyn had never been a legal one; but that Anne could not, under such circumstances, have been guilty of adulterous treason was not deemed to have been a sufficiently important factor to raise complications: the old queen was already dead.

Anne of Cleves succeeded Jane. Even younger than those who had gone before her, she was born in 1515, daughter of the German Duke of Cleves. Henry was attracted to her by a portrait, but when she arrived in England he discovered that she was uncultivated, lacking the refinement of an English or French princess. However, the monarch expressed his determination to proceed with the match, and the two were duly married at Greenwich on January 6, 1540. Henry immediately regretted his impetuousness and set about divorcing Anne, the marriage being terminated six months later, on July 9. His excuse was that he had married Anne against his will, without an 'inward consent to the marriage'. The queen was allowed a pension of £4,000 annually and retired to Chelsea, where she died in 1557. His male heir now secured, the king could well afford to countenance this kind of flippancy; but in all fairness to Anne it was hardly her fault that she could not speak English. A fortnight later Henry married afresh.

This time he set his sights on an English bride, Catherine Howard, daughter of the Duke of Norfolk. But even this match proved of short duration. While Henry made a journey north evidence was accumulated of Catherine's imprudence in the days prior to her marriage. An alliance with the Howard family not being a particularly auspicious factor any longer, Henry decided to dispense with this latest wife also. On a charge of treason, together with her henchwoman, Lady Rochfort, Catherine Howard was beheaded on February 13, 1542, parliament having given its consent. Her father, Norfolk, miraculously retained his position as Lord Treasurer.

opposite:
Katherine Parr, painted by an unknown artist.

The Old Hall, Gainsborough, Lincolnshire. A fine example of early Tudor architecture on a comparatively small scale. It was here in 1540 that Henry VIII met Katherine Parr, then married to a member of the Burgh family.

Henry did not marry for the last time until July 12, 1543. His sixth wife was Katherine Parr, already twice widowed and daughter of Sir Thomas Parr of Kendal, Master of the Wards and Comptroller of the King's Household. Katherine was born in 1513, and was thus thirty at the time of her marriage to Henry, having just received an offer of marriage from Thomas Seymour, brother of the late Queen Jane. Having accepted Seymour's offer, she was informed that the king had already settled on her for his sixth wife. Against her will, she married him.

Although Henry duly attempted to dismiss Katherine in turn, by reacting with intelligence and cunning his new queen escaped the fate of two of her predecessors and outlived her husband, upon whose death she promptly married Thomas Seymour after all, only to die in childbirth at Sudeley Castle in Gloucestershire on September 5, 1548. Buried in the chapel at Sudeley Castle, her remains were not discovered until 1782. An accomplished woman of the world, Katherine was well educated and devoted to several cultural pursuits.

As far as numbers were concerned, Henry exceeded all bounds of propriety in his marriage ventures; but it has to be borne in mind that his earlier marriages all centred about his quest for an heir while those of his later years represented his personal attempts to secure contentment. Always a restless person, Henry could not tolerate dissatisfaction. His marriages had alienated him from so many of his useful acquaintances, and it is no wonder he tended to lack patience.

Henry VIII and Rome

Forasmuch as the King our sovereign lord, perceiving how much the people and subjects of this realm have been vexed, inquieted, and troubled by authorities and jurisdictions legatine in times of the reigns of his noble progenitors, and something touched in his time, to the great diminution and prejudice of the jurisdiction and prerogative royal of this his grace's realms; . . .

His highness therefore straightly chargeth and commandeth that no manner of person of what estate, degree, or condition soever they be of, do pursue or attempt to purchase from the court of Rome or elsewhere, nor use, put in execution, divulge, or publish anything heretofore within this year passed, purchased or to be purchased hereafter, containing matter prejudicial to the high authority, jurisdiction, and prerogative royal of this his said realm, or the let, hindrance, or impeachment of his grace's noble and virtuous intended purposes in the premises, upon pain of incurring the King's high indignation and imprisonment of their bodies for their so doing, and further punishment at his grace's pleasure to the dreadful example of others.

(Proclamation of Henry VIII, prohibiting Papal bulls, Westminster, September 12, 1530).

A good deal of Henry VIII's reign was afflicted by papal problems. His enmity with France led him to defend the papal state militarily; later his alliance with France, although an uneasy one at all times, required him to extend this undertaking. The rise of Wolsey caused ripples of dissension in England; his divorce proceedings against Catherine of Aragon and marriage to Anne Boleyn led to a final and irreparable rupture. The story of the Church of England's origins is largely the story of Henry VIII's personal predicament.

Henry finally broke with Rome during the early 1530's, wholly destroying its influence by the year 1540, dissolving its monasteries, executing those abbots and priors who opposed his will and distributing monastic lands and possessions among his own retainers. One fact, though, should not be overlooked: the break with Rome was a natural circumstance; the Church, despite its immense wealth and the power enjoyed by such of its luminaries as Wolsey, was no more than a useful and heretofore stable European institution. Henry's action, although personally motivated, was a logical and in many ways beneficial action.

In some respects Henry's action can be regarded as a deserved revolutionary gesture, one that accompanied the enlightenment of the Renaissance at a time when people throughout England were questioning Rome's previously un-

Designed by Henry Basse and struck in 1545, this fine medal commemorated Henry VIII's Royal Supremacy of the Church.

challenged authority in so many spheres: a Rome that required much but seemed to return very little. Luther on the continent, Erasmus and More in England; these were principal leaders in the wave of anti-papal feeling; in 1529 Henry VIII added his weight to the general momentum.

The fall of Wolsey, a cleric, and his replacement by More, a layman, was a significant event; Henry's attributed remark, 'If a man should pull down an old stone wall, and begin at the lower part, the upper part thereof might chance to fall upon his head', was no more than a very pertinent observation of fact: before reform of the Church in England might be attempted Rome would have to be deprived of its authority in the realm. Henry affirmed this more solemnly when he declared: 'we are, by the sufferance of God, king of England, and the kings of England in time past never had any superior but God'. His own Commons gave Henry evidence that it too saw much to complain of about the clerical establishment in England. Thereafter Henry personally set about subduing the bishops and their inferiors. When Catherine of Aragon's appeal against his divorcing her was due to be heard in the papal court at Rome, and Pope Clement VII appeared to be employing deliberately delaying tactics, he made the unprecedented suggestion that he was not a subject of the Pope and was therefore quite different from other European monarchs who, although they might complain, never disputed the Pope's authority. Henry followed this by demanding that the legality of his divorce should be decided by an English ecclesiastical court, not one at Rome.

Naturally the Pope questioned Henry's assertions. Henry countered, as he had done from the outset, by asking university dons and accredited scholars of all complexions to ascertain precedents, potential loopholes and indeed any vestige of learning that could be utilised in order to support his contentions: firstly, that he was within his rights to divorce Catherine, and secondly, that the Pope's jurisdiction in England was in practice no more than nominal. Henry capped his endeavours in this field by announcing himself not merely king but 'emperor', with regnal powers invested in him personally rather than in his inherited office. To substantiate his claims he instigated enquiries into four separate questions he wished to stress: all reference to 'authority imperial' ascribed to the English crown; whether papal authority in matters matrimonial was of recent origin or rooted in antiquity; whether Henry was answerable to the Vatican in any matters other than those surrounding heresy; and lastly, all previous references to papal interference in royal divorce and marriage in England. Henry's two scholars — Benet and Carne — had been set an almost impossible task, especially as their researches had to be carried out among the Vatican archives, with as much secrecy as possible but under the observation of the Pope's own servants. Not unnaturally they discovered nothing, time also being against them in their Herculean labour.

In January, 1531 Henry went a step further. He had already indicted certain of his bishops on charges of lesser treason; now he indicted the whole clerical body in England, on the charge that, collectively, it had illegally administered papal law within the realm. The clergy immediately sought pardon for transgressions — though on no apparent authority — and the charge was withdrawn. Ever one to consider his treasury in all his undertakings, Henry extorted as much as £100,000 from the southern convocation, the first to beg his pardon. Next Henry demanded recognition of his title of 'Defender of the Faith' being amended to 'Protector and only Supreme Head of the English Church', which was something quite different. The clergy, though, did not acquiesce easily, and many alterations were made to Henry's suggested ecclesiastical powers.

Serious wranglings followed at Rome, both about Henry's new insistence upon personal supremacy and about the matter of Queen Catherine's appeal. In June, 1531 Henry made his position quite clear: 'Even if his holiness should do his worst by excommunicating me and so forth, I shall not mind it, for I care not a fig for all his excommunications'. Henry's path towards 'Royal Supremacy' had now, as this statement asserted, been laid down concretely. Only time, and the ironing out of immediate difficulties, would be required in order to implement the new order. Events continued in their own unsatisfactory way for many months; Thomas Cranmer was appointed Archbishop of Canterbury on March 30, 1533; and finally, on July 11, 1533, Pope Clement VII formally excommunicated the English king.

Considerations of space preclude the documentation of the final events leading up to this excommunication and the establishment of supremacy, but the initiatory points have been given here. As far as England was concerned this was one of the most significant domestic changes of any era. Henry may have proceeded blindly towards the final result, relied more upon heat of temper and stubborness than proper reason; his motives may only have been personal, tempered with greed; but the establishment of an English Church was a truly momentous action, the reform long overdue. Henry's authority in England was confirmed in 1534, when parliament introduced an act requiring all men to take an oath upholding Henry's marriage to Anne Boleyn and rejecting the authority of the Pope who had declared the marriage invalid. Such men as More, who refused to take this oath, were threatened with execution.

The dissolution of the monasteries

. . . For so soon as the visitors were entered within the gates, they called the abbot and other officers of the house and caused them to deliver all the keys, and took an inventory of all their goods, both within doors and without. For all such beasts, horses, sheep and such cattle as were abroad in pasture or grange places, the visitors caused to be brought into their presence. And when they had done so, they turned the abbot and all his convent and household forth of the doors. But such persons as afterwards bought their corn or hay or such like, finding all the doors either open or the locks and shackles plucked down, went in and took what they found and filched it away.

(Manuscript in the British Museum).

When Henry VIII decided to dissolve the monasteries in England and Wales (he was unable to persuade the Scots king to follow suit at the time) he was in fact carrying out two distinct operations. Firstly he was completing the task he had set himself when he separated from Rome, whose sway in English monastic establishments was still very strong. Secondly he set out to replenish his own coffers at the expense not so much of the Church, but rather of a group of people who had in recent years been described as pariahs, living off the fat of the land

and the exertions of people less well placed than themselves. He accomplished
this latter not so much by the seizure of monastic treasures — although he did
this, at the same time providing for pensions to be granted to those monks who
offered no resistance to the requirements of his representatives, or 'visitors' —
but by granting monastic lands and buildings to people of his own choosing,
exacting due payment from them for their newly acquired property.

That Henry probably felt some alarm at the power of monasticism in
England may be deduced from the fact that when he came to the throne there
were altogether about 900 residential religious houses in the country. Admittedly some of these were no more than 'cells', but several housed more than a
hundred men or women and were immensely wealthy, drawing vast incomes
from the local populace through monastic tithes. Certain abbots of larger

establishments had been mitred, thereby being placed on the same footing as bishops and some of them earning a place in the House of Lords.

In attacking these medieval religious houses — many of which dated back to the eleventh century and earlier — Henry undoubtedly felt he had much justification; at the same time he effectively brought to an end the practice of one of England's finest art forms, the illumination of manuscripts, as well as a considerable concentration of contemporary historical and literary activity. The introduction of printing and the scholarly activity at Oxford and Cambridge in some manner made up for Henry's emphatic actions, while the blossoming of miniature painting during Elizabeth's reign replaced the ecclesiastical art of illumination.

The most unfortunate accompaniment of Henry's action was the violence that was seen as necessary upon occasion. Perhaps most notable of all such instances was the hanging on Glastonbury Tor of the abbot, Richard Whyting, who had refused to surrender to the king's men voluntarily. Numerous such examples occurred throughout the country.

The history of the dissolution can be traced from the year 1535, when a survey was made of the wealth of English monasteries and churches, the end product being entitled 'Valor Ecclesiasticus'. From this report Henry was enabled to decide the order in which houses should be closed: as it happened the 'lesser' monasteries, those assessed at an annual value of £200 or less, came first. That this survey was carried out by four men over a period of just a few months is some indication of how undefinitive it must have been. Actual dissolution began the following year, with the passing of an 'Act for the Suppression of the Lesser Monasteries'. This process was carried out quite humanely, inmates of these smaller houses being allowed the choice either of entering another, larger house of their own selection or of being freed from their religious vows to pursue a secular career. The royal 'visitors' of 1535 had roundly declared upon the lack of moral obedience and devotion in the religious houses they had inspected, giving Henry every excuse for their closure; however, this initial campaign which closed down only 243 houses during the spring and summer of 1536 caused very little hardship and could hardly be regarded as the overture to a mass destruction of monasticism in England. As far as the general population who witnessed this move was concerned, all that was involved was the transfer of monastic lands (and with them several secular jobs, domestic and agricultural) from one employer to another.

The second stage of the dissolution likewise appeared to presage only the pruning of monasticism. It began as the direct result of the so-called 'Pilgrimage of Grace', a rebellion which took place in the north during October, 1536 and an expression of general discontent on many levels that was only spurred by the act of dissolution. The rebels regained several dissolved houses and invited the dispossessed inhabitants to return, which many did; but when the king moved against the rebels, utterly breaking their cause, the returned religious had to abandon their homes once more.

For certain 'greater' abbeys and priories which had backed the rebels danger lay ahead, and five of their abbots were executed for treason. Furness Abbey in Lancashire provided Henry with his principal lever to the next stage of dissolution; for here, although no positive charges could be brought against them, many of the monks had sympathised with the rebels and their position was now very much compromised. The quandary was resolved by the abbot voluntarily surrendering his properties to the king. Other abbots began to follow his example when pressure was applied upon them to do so, although it was only in November, 1537, when the Cluniac priory at Lewes surrendered to Henry's men, that this procession began, and by early 1538 others were following suit in gradually increasing numbers. The last abbey to surrender, in March, 1540, was at Waltham, and with its succumbence active monasticism in

England came practically to a close; as far as Henry was concerned no monks or nuns remained. Many of these surrenders, although technically 'voluntary', were only achieved by a good deal of bargaining; even so, the so-called 'Second Suppression Act' of 1539 was hardly necessary, being introduced as a formality to legalise an already achieved circumstance.

Naturally Henry incurred a good deal of ill will as his policies were carried out, and in retrospect much of what he did was unduly harsh. On the other hand reform of some kind was long overdue, and its dire effect on a minority hardly affected the majority of his subjects at all. Many of the 10,000 monks, nuns and other religious found places in the established Church, not a few appear to have been glad of the opportunity to renounce their vows in any case, and only a very small number indeed became the wandering beggars, burdens on their fellow men, that Henry's denigrators suggested. Of the properties thus affected most crumbled into the 'picturesque' ruins which are now so carefully preserved. Roof leading was stripped away in order to manufacture cannon balls, church bells were melted down to manufacture cannon, and stones from the structures themselves were slowly removed by local builders for their own properties. Henry created six new cathedrals following the dissolution, and these are virtually the only monastic churches to have survived in any degree of completeness: Bristol, Chester, Gloucester, Oxford, Peterborough and Westminster (the latter being subsequently deprived of its cathedral status). Such remarkable cathedral buildings as Durham, Ely, Lincoln and Wells had enjoyed their status since medieval times. A few domestic monastic buildings also survived when their new owners converted them into manor houses. But by and large Henry's action was decisive and emphatic.

Thomas Cromwell

'... And thus much will I say to you, that I intend, God willing, this afternoon, when my lord hath dined, to ride to London, and so to the court, where I will either make or mar or I come again. I will put myself in the press, to see what any man is able to lay to my charge of untruth or misdemeanour'.

(The young Cromwell to George Cavendish, from Cavendish's *Life of Cardinal Wolsey*).

If Thomas Wolsey had been the most powerful minister during the early part of Henry VIII's reign, Thomas Cromwell, later Earl of Essex, certainly occupied an equal position during a later period in his monarch's reign. Born about 1490 in Putney, he differed from Wolsey in not being a cleric. He was the son of a blacksmith and his early education but slight; his first employment was in the office of a merchant at Antwerp. From there he travelled into Italy, returning to England about 1527 in order to study law and enjoy the patronage of Wolsey. It was indeed in the latter's downfall that the ambitious Cromwell's good fortune was kindled. He was called to Wolsey's defence in the House of

previous page:

Rievaulx Abbey, Yorkshire, perhaps one of the finest of all religious houses to suffer dissolution. A Cistercian foundation dating from 1132, it had at one time boasted some 600 inhabitants, although numbers gradually fell over the years. It was closed in 1538.

Commons, was noticed by the alert Henry and rapidly saw preferment, being appointed Henry's private secretary and a Privy Councillor and knighted in 1531. In 1534 he was elevated to the office of Chief Secretary of State and Master of the Rolls; in 1535 he became Visitor-General of the English monasteries and finally, in 1536, Keeper of the Great Seal. The Earldom of Essex was bestowed upon him in 1539, together with some thirty monastic manors and lands which he had been instrumental in seizing; at the same time he was created Lord Chamberlain.

His fall came just as suddenly and mercurially as his rise. For purely political ends he had encouraged the match between Henry and Anne of Cleves; in the final analysis the match proved to be unnecessary, while Henry himself realised he could not tolerate Anne the moment he set eyes on her. On June 10, 1540 Cromwell was arrested in retribution. The following month parliament annulled Henry's latest marriage and on July 28 Cromwell was beheaded at Tyburn. That Henry then married the Catholic Catherine Howard caused many observers to deduce that a return to Rome was being heralded now that Cromwell had gone, but Henry of course had no such intention.

Cromwell's error was probably to take for granted that his numerous actions to the benefit of the crown would earn him unqualified gratitude and immunity from subsequent indictment. Admittedly the royal finances had been vastly improved by the dissolution of the monasteries, carried out under Cromwell's supervision, and equally the statesman had been diligent in establishing Henry's personal might, but the king was not one to entertain notions of inalienable patronage for his subordinates. He was cunning in allowing others to undertake demanding work on his behalf, but only for as long as he wished and no longer, and thus he would not willingly allow Cromwell to overstep the bounds of his allotted authority. Earl of Essex he may have been, but that did not grant him the right to assume power over the king. His arranging the disastrous Anne of Cleves match was but one incident, an example of the kind of sway he felt himself to possess; in itself it was not the main cause of Henry's anger, but it provided convenient justification to oust the over-powerful statesman.

In some ways Cromwell's downfall was a tragedy. He was no more corrupt in amassing wealth than anyone else in high office at that time; he had even gone so far as to make personal provision for the London poor. Nor for that matter did he accumulate as many riches during his lifetime as many assumed he would have done. That he appeared cowardly when faced with execution probably stemmed only from his fear of the preliminary tortures and mutilations that preceded the execution of all traitors not of noble stock (noblemen being executed in the Tower), which Cromwell was not allowed to be, despite his elevation to the peerage.

Cranmer, who was himself to meet a more frightful death before long, was one of those who came forward to Cromwell's defence. The deposed statesman, he wrote to Henry, was 'such a servant in my judgement, in wisdom, diligence, faithfulness, and experience, as no prince in this realm ever had'. It is not an unworthy epitaph on the unfortunate Cromwell, though it contradicts the suggestion often put forward that his true mistake was not so much that he over-applied himself to matters of politics, but rather that in so doing he failed to take into account the common rules of tact and diplomacy.

Thomas Cromwell medal of 1538.

The hall at Christ Church, Oxford. This photograph illustrates effectively the fine hammer-beam roof typical of early Tudor architecture.

Learning and the Arts under Henry VIII

Our king does not desire gold or gems or precious metals, but virtue, glory, immortality.... The other day he wished he was more learned. I said, that is not what we expect of your Grace, but that you will foster and encourage learned men. Yea, surely, said he, for indeed without them we should scarcely exist at all.

(Letter received by Erasmus).

Henry possessed many faults and was on occasion lascivious, tyrannical or unthinking; he was nevertheless a man of pronounced general culture and a ready patron of the arts. During his reign the arts flourished, paving the way for the coming artistic marvels of his daughter Elizabeth's reign. The translation of the Bible is dealt with elsewhere, but many other exciting publishing events are associated with Henry's time, perhaps the most notable of all being the publication in 1511 of Erasmus' *In Praise of Folly*. The first complete

Henry VIII was an accomplished musician, and this illustration from his own psalter depicts him playing the harp. In attendance is his famous jester, Will Somers. He had been introduced to Henry in 1525 and thereafter enjoyed the close confidence of his monarch, witnessing the passing of many favourites over the years but himself remaining in favour. Towards the end of Henry's life Somers became especially close to his master and was often the only person capable of cheering him up. He also enjoyed the friendship of Wolsey. In order to mock courtly manners pointedly, he frequently carried a monkey about with him. Unlike lesser jesters, Somers was kept in the background of Henry's life and was rarely required to entertain publicly.

Trinity College, Cambridge. This
view of the great court shows the
Tudor gatehouses common to
academic institutions at the time.

edition of Chaucer's works saw the light of day in 1532; while such miscellaneous publications as John Skelton's *Colyn Cloute*, in which the clergy was
blamed for England's troubles, are still capable of providing interest.

It was during the reign of Henry VIII also that courtiers, emulating the
French, began to deem it an essential accomplishment to be able to write
verses. Like so much other cultural activity this fashion was carried to a state
of excellence during the reign of Elizabeth. Henry himself wrote poetry, as well
as accomplished melodies.

Among several important historical works to have appeared during Henry's
reign was Polydore Vergil's Latin *Anglica Historia* of 1534, recording the
history of England down to the death of Henry VII (and in a later edition
carrying the story down to 1537), and Edward Hall's *Chronicle*. Hall died in
1547, but his book was not published in its entirety until 1550, the earlier part
having appeared in 1532. He was a fervent admirer of Henry VIII, and his
writing amply mirrors this fact.

Scholarship and learning also made considerable advances. Henry himself
was the benefactor of certain colleges, founding Trinity College, Cambridge, in
1546 and re-founding Christ Church, Oxford, in 1532 (this latter had been
originally founded by Wolsey in 1525 under the name of Cardinal College). As
was common at the time, founders and benefactors of colleges emblazoned the
gatehouses of their foundations with their coats of arms and frequently also
with stone carved representations of themselves. Such a statue of Henry exists
over the gateway of Trinity College, Cambridge, while the Tudor rose is
prominently displayed above the gateway of Christ's College in the same city,
founded in 1505 by Archbishop Fisher and Margaret Beaufort, Henry VII's
mother, who is depicted in sculpted form.

Although learning blossomed at the universities and numerous men of note
attended them, men like Wolsey kept a strict watch for 'heretical' opinions that
it was felt might be fostered in these institutions. Greek came into popularity as

opposite:

Tudor wood carving. Part of a panel
from a house at Waltham Abbey
dating from the third decade of the
sixteenth century. Notable for the
early assimilation of Italian
Renaissance traits, this detail
illustrates various decorative heads
and armorial bearings.

an academic discipline, but from time to time it was officially frowned upon because of the free-thinking sentiments of certain of the ancient Greek writers (and because the New Testament had been originally written in Greek and its re-interpretation was feared). With the removal of Wolsey there were others who maintained a watch over the direction of academic activity in England, to re-direct it should certain trends appear dangerous all of a sudden. Henry himself, by overseeing all senior appointments in the universities (at one time Thomas More was High Steward at both Oxford and Cambridge), kept close control over their policies. When the prolonged divorce proceedings against Catherine of Aragon were in progress, and scholars were required to undertake research on the king's behalf in order to glean precedents and learned opinions, he more or less directed the activities of the two principal places of learning.

Numerous new chairs were created at both Oxford and Cambridge; by way of contrast the dissolution of the religious houses caused many severances of one-time ties between ecclesiastical institutions and certain of the colleges; while the few monastic colleges in England, at Durham, Canterbury and elsewhere, were automatically swept away. This break in ecclesiastical academic pursuit caused a reduction in the numbers of those following wholly religious studies — and a consequent increase in the popularity of other disciplines, including civil law and medicine — and a greater preponderance of wealthy young men who attended the universities for largely social reasons. In this respect learning can be said to have suffered during Henry's reign. Conversely, the list of eminent scholars produced by Oxford and Cambridge at this time is impressive enough, including William Tyndale from Oxford and Robert Ascham, William Cecil and Stephen Gardiner from Cambridge, among many others. Of the numerous books of a speculative or scholarly kind published during Henry's reign may be cited Elyot's *Governour* (1531), More's *Utopia* (1516), Tyndale's *Obedience of a Christian Man* (1528) and of course Tyndale's famous translation of the New Testament of 1526 (printed in Germany).

The pictorial arts were extensively patronised during Henry's reign also, most markedly however under foreign influence. The most significant painter active in England at the time was undoubtedly Hans Holbein, born in Augsburg in 1494. He settled in Basel at about the age of twenty and there succeeded in making a living as an illustrator, at the same time undertaking commissions for oil portraits in several parts of Switzerland. It was at Basel that he encountered Erasmus, who asked him to provide the illustrations for *In Praise of Folly*. Several years later, in 1526, after Holbein had met with notable success on the continent, it was Erasmus also who persuaded him to travel to England, giving him letters of introduction to such men as Thomas More. For almost three years Holbein lodged in More's London residence and painted English men and women of note, almost all of them friends or relatives of the author of *Utopia*.

Thereafter success was assured, especially after Holbein found favour with the king (which was probably about 1534, although one source assigns the occasion to a much earlier date, claiming that Henry visited More and was immediately struck by Holbein's paintings). In the meantime the painter had revisited Switzerland, discovered that fortune came to him more readily in London and returned to the English capital. Appointed painter to the court, he received such miscellaneous commissions as a visit to Cleves in 1539 in order to portray the Princess Anne, his portrait winning the king's approval. That Henry subsequently rejected Anne seems not to have caused Holbein any hardship at all, even though it cost Thomas Cromwell his head. The artist returned to Basel once again, its citizens offering him a pension to remain in their midst. Holbein turned the offer down and returned to the prosperity he had known at the English court, and he died in England in 1543.

opposite:
A golden grace cup presented by Henry VIII to the Company of Barber Surgeons of London, in whose possession it still is. Henry was keenly interested in the progress of medicine in his time and in 1518 had presented a charter to the College of Physicians of London. By an act of 1540 physicians were allowed to practise surgery; but the same act prevented barbers from undertaking surgery, which had led to considerable abuse in the past. A separate charter was presented to the Barber Surgeons (incorporated in the fourteenth century) in 1541. An ancient trade guild, it was one of many existing in the City of London.

Holbein's portraiture was perhaps the most accomplished to be witnessed in England until the eighteenth century. In that he painted so many important people who lived during the latter part of Henry VIII's reign he could lay claim to being a contemporary historian of more than passing value. He had many followers and a 'School of Holbein' rapidly came into existence; but it is significant that it lasted no longer than the early years of Elizabeth I's reign, when an entirely new kind of portraiture came into being.

William Tyndale and the translation of the Bible

. . . it was ordained and commanded amongst other things that in all and singular parish churches there should be provided by a certain day, now expired, at the costs of the curates and parishioners, Bibles containing the Old and New Testament in the English tongue, . . .

And notwithstanding the King's said most godly and gracious commandment and injunction in form as is aforesaid, his royal majesty is informed that divers and many towns and parishes within this realm have negligently omitted their duties in the accomplishment thereof; whereof his highness marveleth not a little. And minding the execution of his said former most godly and gracious injunctions, doth straightly charge and command that the curates and parishioners of every town and parish within this his realm of England, not having already Bibles provided within their parish churches, shall on this side of the Feast of All Saints next coming, buy and provide Bibles of the largest and greatest volume, and cause the same to be set and fixed in every of the said parish churches, there to be used as aforesaid according to the said former injunctions.

And finally, the King's royal majesty doth declare and signify to all and singular his loving subjects, that to the intent they may have the said Bibles of the greatest volume at equal and reasonable prices, his highness by the advice of his council, hath ordained and taxed that the sellers thereof shall not take for any of the said Bibles, unbound, above the price of 10s. And for every of the said Bibles well and sufficiently bound, trimmed, and clasped, not above 12s., . .

(Proclamation of Henry VIII, Waltham, May 6, 1541).

An engraving of the New Jerusalem from the 1536 edition of Tyndale's translation of the New Testament.

Born in 1484, the year before Henry VII's victory on Bosworth Field, William Tyndale published his English translation of the New Testament in 1526. This he achieved in Germany, where he was living in exile after discovering that the English clergy were antagonistic towards his own reformed doctrines. His translation did however win him new friends in England; although Tunstall, then Bishop of London, bought up all copies he could trace of the new work and burned them, the efficient Wolsey presiding over his bonfire. Nor did Tyndale's fortunes improve thereafter. In 1534 and 1535 successively he published two new editions of his work, but during the latter year was arrested at Antwerp, imprisoned for sixteen months and then publicly strangled and burnt at Vilvorde on October 6, 1536. His offence had been to attempt to bring the gospel story more readily before the English people.

Tyndale had been notorious for his polemical works for some time prior to the publication of this translation, but it was his translation above all else that was taken by many as an example of sacrilege, especially as he observed no reverence for long-established connotations of certain passages, frequently translating one Greek word in several different ways. His onerous earlier reputation stood against him and his work was automatically forbidden. Within thirteen years of his New Testament's publication and after his own death Tyndale's translation was however accepted throughout England, though in a different guise and under a different ascription than originally. It was in September, 1538 that Thomas Cromwell, in Henry's name, ordered that a large-size English translation of the Bible be placed in every parish church in England and that congregations should be encouraged to read it. The version Cromwell stipulated should be distributed was that published by William Coverdale in 1535; however, Cranmer came across a different translation, dedicated to the king by one Thomas Matthew (whose true name was John Rogers). The beginning of the Old Testament in this version, together with all of the New Testament, was in fact Tyndale's. This edition provided the text for the official Bible introduced to churches in 1539.

Tyndale could not of course play any part in the distribution of this Bible; his earlier activity had however been an essential component in the process leading up to this event and it was fitting that his translation should be adopted. On a wider plane, an English translation was long overdue: Luther's German translation of the New Testament had been completed as long ago as 1522, and indeed Tyndale had referred to this when undertaking his own translation. As a part of the general Renaissance movement it was virtually inevitable. In that Tyndale's translation was the first in English, and unbeknown to his detractors eventually found its way to official acceptance, it has earned a lasting place in the history of both English literature and the English Church.

The troubles with Scotland

The King our sovereign lord, being certainly advised that the Duke of Albany is of late descended and arrived in Scotland having great number and provision of men of war, Scots and others, with artillery and ordnance, intending to invade this the King's realm the morrow after St. Luke's Day next coming, straightly chargeth and commandeth all and singular his subjects of every estate, degree and condition within the said county of Stafford, . . .that they forthwith put themselves in such assured and perfect a readiness as, upon one day's warning to be sent to them by the King's said Lieutenant, they may (all excuses and delays utterly set apart) proceed and set forth with all diligence toward such places as they shall be appointed unto for the service of war to be done against the King's said enemies the Scots and others. . . .

(Proclamation of Henry VIII, Hampton Court, October 10, 1523).

Although the 'auld alliance' dating from 1295 between Scotland and France tended throughout the reigns of Henry VII and Henry VIII to link the various disagreements between England and both Scotland and France, in fact they were two distinct problems. Ever since Roman times, when it had been found necessary to construct Hadrian's Wall in order to keep the northerners at bay, there had been border squabbles between the Scots and the people dwelling in northern England. As mentioned elsewhere, James IV had married Margaret Tudor, Henry VII's daughter, in 1503, but this served in no way to create a lasting bond between the two kingdoms. Tension was evident throughout the latter years of Henry VII's reign, but with the accession of Henry VIII this tension became ever more pronounced, even though the new monarch renewed his father's 1502 treaty with Scotland on June 29, 1510.

Following the death of Henry VII in 1509 Margaret Tudor had inherited certain jewellery, which her brother duly refused to hand over to her. This did not help in creating good relations; it was followed in 1510 by Sir Edward Howard's killing Andrew Barton, one of James IV's favourites, and making off with two of his ships, the *Lion* and the *Jenett of Purwyn*. Although Barton was looked upon as partly piratical in his dealings, Howard's action naturally incurred the Scottish monarch's anger, his temper being rendered even less equable by Henry's refusing to consider any form of compensation. Seeking papal authority to do so, James denounced his treaty with England and threatened war, though he had no real desire to pursue this course (being brother-in-law to the English monarch and having a good claim to succeed to the English crown, Henry still being without legitimate male issue).

Foreign affairs occupied the attentions of both monarchs. James IV died in 1513, to be succeeded by the infant James V, Henry VIII's nephew. It was at this time that John Stewart, Earl of Albany and cousin to James V (also his heir at that moment), travelled to Scotland and succeeded in driving Margaret, then wed to the Earl of Angus, across the border into England, thereby personally insulting the English ruler. Over the ensuing years Albany made every effort to raise a Scots army and attack England, but without success, and in 1522 Wolsey ordered the Scots to expel him. On October 25 Albany sailed for France (against whom England was then contemplating an attack), Henry offering the Scots a sixteen year truce providing he would remain abroad. Henry also hinted at a marriage between James V and his own daughter, the Princess Mary (who was then betrothed to Charles V).

The Scots easily perceived the flippant nature of Henry's suggestions, turned them down out of hand and for their action were subjected to an English attack under the leadership of Thomas Howard, Earl of Surrey. The entire Scots border underwent devastation as a result; Kelso and Jedburgh were both burnt; but the Scottish troops avoided defeat and the English suffered severe losses. Albany, returning from France, actually launched a counter-attack against Surrey, but failed because his own troops refused to advance. On May 24, 1524 Albany left Scotland.

This particular English expedition was futile. Fortunately Albany's exit lessened French influence in the northern kingdom and a respite from hostilities became possible. James V was proclaimed king in his own right and Margaret now received strong intimations that Henry really would allow his daughter Mary to marry the young Scottish monarch.

Henry's activities elsewhere led to further new developments, and in May, 1533 England and Scotland signed a truce at Newcastle, transformed into a permanent treaty the year following. As far as the English monarch was concerned, this procured him a new ally in his quarrel with the Vatican. James was wooed further by being honoured with the Order of the Garter, and of course there remained the promise of Mary's hand in marriage. This last James himself negated on January 1, 1537 when he married Madeleine of France, but still Henry affected friendship for his nephew. James further tested his uncle's good will by marrying Mary of Guise in June, 1538 following Madeleine's sudden death: noted for her good looks, this same princess had already been suggested as a possible wife to Henry himself.

For a short while peace reigned. Henry was principally occupied with annexing monastic lands, and the Scottish question only re-arose when he suggested that James V should follow suit and dissolve the Scottish monasteries. A meeting, with a view to discussing this proposal, was scheduled for September, 1541 in York. Henry duly travelled there, in majestic splendour with a huge retinue, despatching heavy pieces of artillery to the northern city by boat. He left his capital in the care of only a handful of ministers, and even took with him his new queen (Catherine Howard) and his daughter Mary. He paused at every town on the way, his following of 5,000 horse establishing what at each place was virtually a military camp, consisting of some 200 tents and pavilions. All in all Henry took four months over the journey to and from York, only to discover at York, bent as he was upon displaying to the Yorkists that his might was now greater than ever, that the Scottish monarch had slighted him and not travelled south.

The 78 days it took to reach York were scheduled according to a pre-determined timetable. It was the first time Henry had travelled this far north and his journey was not therefore wasted; his royal progress allowed thousands of his subjects to see their monarch, to perceive his greatness and to admire the beauty of his queen and the solidarity of his accompanying courtiers and soldiers. It also proved to every interested observer of English affairs that the Tudor king was in a sufficiently strong position to leave the south of England for an extended period without fear of treachery during his absence. This feeling of strength was illustrated even more potently in the revenge he took over James V for not honouring his appointment.

He did not attack the Scots at once, but passed the winter and first half of 1542 in making preparations. In August, 1542 Sir Robert Bowes launched the attack. He was defeated at Haddon Rig, leading Henry to declare in defence that it had been the Scots who had begun hostilities. This was followed by an offensive under the leadership of Thomas Howard, now Duke of Norfolk, who was ordered by his monarch to take Edinburgh. The duke was responsible for the razing of several Scottish towns en route, but he was finally let down by his own men who were short of food and drink and utterly wearied by their fighting and the Scottish counter-attacks. He returned to England defeated.

James V immediately decided on revenge. He despatched two armies, one travelling south from the east and the other from the west. Both were successfully repulsed by the harassed English. Then on December 14 the sick Scottish monarch died, ashamed over the huge losses he had suffered in this counter-offensive. He was succeeded on the throne by the baby girl, Mary, born only six days previously. To the English king this was a favourable circumstance, giving a hint of lasting peace between the two countries: for firstly England had just succeeded in humbling Scotland, and secondly the northern kingdom was now without a satisfactory sovereign.

Though he was grieved by the heir apparent, Arran being appointed regent to the baby Mary, Henry's immediate suggestion was to arrange a betrothal between his own son and heir, Edward, and Mary. At Holyrood House, on August 25, 1543 a treaty to this effect was in fact ratified and at this time it appeared as though Henry had won Scotland for his own, that the monasteries there would be dissolved and that Rome would be banished altogether from Great Britain. In this he was mistaken. Seizing Scottish ships in the Thames and presenting himself as master of the Scots in every way, he caused only disgruntlement. In 1544 the Scottish parliament nullified the treaty with England. In retaliation Henry sent Edward Seymour, Earl of Hertford (created

Henry VIII in old age, from a rare print of an engraving after Cornelius Matsys' drawing of 1544. In making the engraving the later hand has reversed the original drawing, and thus the artist's initials and date read in reverse.

Duke of Somerset in 1547) to take revenge on the Scots. He landed at Newhaven on May 4, 1544, burned Edinburgh, destroyed Holyrood House and hit Leith badly. Marching south, Hertford continued with his policy of destruction, but the only effect it had was to engender an even more resolute intent in Scottish hearts to take revenge on the English. Henry's betrothal of his niece Margaret (daughter of his sister Margaret by the Earl of Arran) to Matthew, Earl of Lennox, further enraged Scotland. At Ancrum, on February 27, 1545, the Scots defeated the English decisively, their leader being Margaret's one-time husband, Angus. Thereafter, until the time of Henry VIII's death, complete confusion and continued squabbling characterised English-Scottish relations. Certain Scottish monasteries were destroyed by English troops, and Archbishop Beaton of St. Andrews, long an opponent of Henry's religious activities, was murdered in his castle, possibly at the instigation of England. With Henry's death and the withdrawl of English ships from the Scottish coastline (his naval superiority being Henry's greatest strength) hostilities were brought to a close.

Henry VIII's children

The Year of our Lord 1537, was a Prince born to King Henry *the 8th, by* Jane Seimour *then Queen; who within a few days after the Birth of her Son, died, and was buried at the Castle of* Windsor. *This Child was Christned by the Duke of* Norfolk, *the Duke of* Suffolk, *and the Arch-Bishop of* Canterbury. *Afterwards was brought up till he came to six Years old among the Women. At the sixth Year of his Age he was brought up in Learning by Master Doctor* Cox, *who was after his Almoner, and* John Cheeke *Master of Arts, two well-learned Men, who fought to bring him up in learning of Tongues, of the Scripture, of Philosophy, and all Liberal Sciences. . . . The tenth Year not yet ended, it was appointed he should be created Prince of* Wales, *Duke of* Cornwal, *and Count Palatine of* Chester: *At which time, being the Year of our Lord 1547, the said King died of a Dropsie as it was thought. After whose death incontinent came* Edward *Earl of* Hartford, *and Sir* Anthony Brown *Master of the Horse, to convoy this Prince to* Enfield, *where the Earl of* Hartford *declared to him, and his younger sister* Elizabeth, *the Death of their Father.*

(From Edward VI's *Journal).*

Much of the tragedy of Henry VIII's reign stemmed from his desire to provide himself with a legitimate male offspring. He did finally succeed in this, and in fathering two daughters who like their brother were destined to occupy the English throne. Eldest of the three was Mary, daughter of his first wife, Catherine of Aragon, and born at Greenwich on February 8, 1516. She was however but one of a number of children Henry could have wished to survive

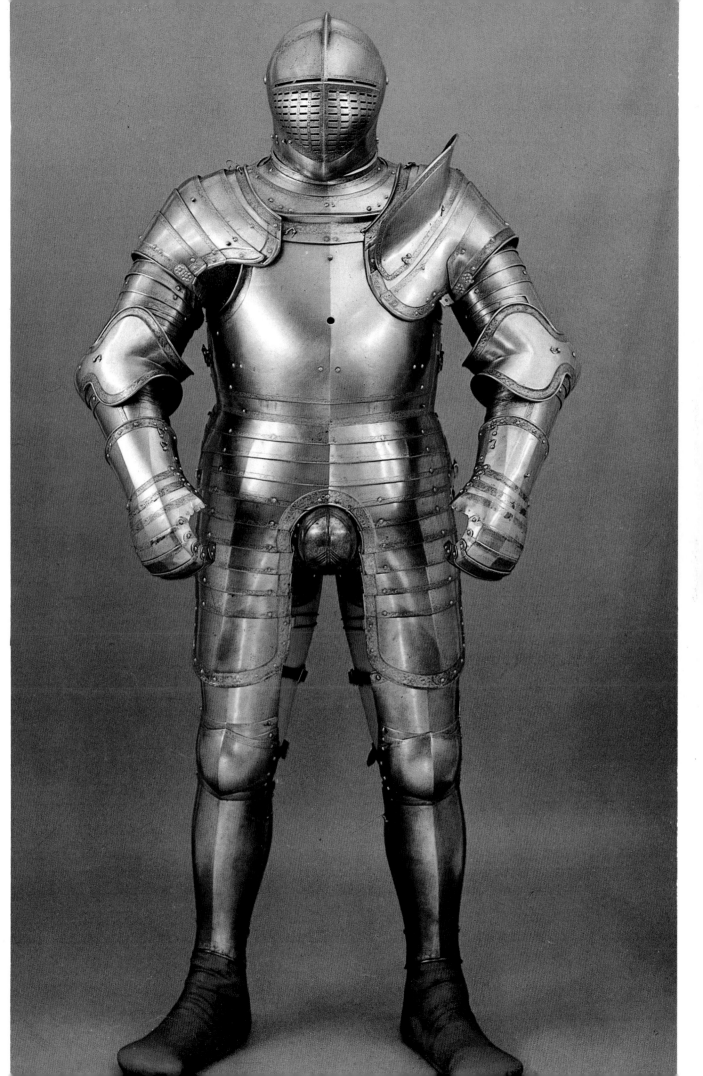

opposite:
The Princess Elizabeth. A lovely
painting by an unknown artist of
the future queen. Richly habited,
the studious Elizabeth is
appropriately shown with her books.
When she became queen, Elizabeth
was in the habit of placing books in
convenient places about her rooms
with the intention that her courtiers
should read them.

from his union with his first wife, but unhappily Catherine suffered several miscarriages as well as three still-births, two of which were boys. Even more tragic were the deaths of two other of her babies, one a boy and one a girl, only a matter of weeks following their births. Lacking brothers and sisters, therefore, and with a mother who had been rejected by her father, Mary herself knew only a somewhat unpleasant childhood. Added to her other misfortunes was the fact that at the whim of an impetuous father she could be betrothed to any European or Scottish prince he cared to select for her, according only to the diplomatic circumstances of the hour.

Because he required his first marriage to be declared null, Henry when he divorced Catherine was left without a legitimate heir, either male or female. His marriage to Anne Boleyn was thus doubly important to him. Since he particularly hoped for a son, the birth of the Princess Elizabeth was a great disappointment when it occurred at Greenwich on September 7, 1533. With the execution of her mother and consequent annulment of her claim to the throne Elizabeth could look forward only to a childhood even bleaker than that of her half-sister Mary. For several years she lived isolated from her family at Hatfield House in Hertfordshire.

Both daughters were rejected by their father, their upbringing placed in the hands of ladies in waiting. The 'illegitimate' Mary was obliged upon the birth of Elizabeth to assume second place in public importance to her young relative, and in order to effect this circumstance the princess was subjected to considerable insult. Perhaps most humiliating to her was not being allowed to attend mass for fear the congregations should accord her a due recognition of her status. She was obliged to alter her dwelling places with great frequency and was forbidden contact either with her father or her mother.

However, being a daughter of Aragon and possessing contacts overseas she was able to some extent to keep in touch with the outside world; she even succeeded in despatching personal letters to the Pope. The Emperor Charles, who took up her cause and went so far as to promote matches on her behalf, finally set plans in motion to secure her escape, though Henry managed to frustrate them. After Catherine of Aragon's death Mary once again attempted reconciliation with her father, but he would hear of it only if she would swear the oath required of his subjects acknowledging his supremacy and in addition her own illegitimacy. Her governess Lady Hussey removed to the Tower, Cromwell himself fearing for his office for having championed her cause, the unhappy princess was finally forced to submit to her father's wishes, conceding that Henry's marriage to Catherine of Aragon had been incestuous. However, having signed her father's document without even reading it, she sought the Pope's absolution for her unwilling act.

When Henry married Katherine Parr, his last wife, his two daughters and Prince Edward were united for the first time and Mary was at last restored to her position of seniority over Elizabeth. For the first time in their lives Henry VIII's two daughters experienced attentiveness, both to their education and their general well-being; they experienced also the blessings of security.

Edward was born at Hampton Court on October 12, 1537, his mother Jane Seymour dying as a result of his birth. With this prince's appearance Henry's ambition was realised: the Tudor line would be perpetuated on the male side. Naturally a prince of this consquence was assured of being given every attention during his infancy and youth, even to the point of being unduly sheltered; unfortunately the king was not to live long enough to ensure his son's protection for a sufficient period of time.

A frail child from the start, such protection was of course doubly important. Edward's food was specially prepared and for the first six years of his life he lived exclusively among the womenfolk of the court. Even at this early stage of his life, though, he enjoyed the benefit of a large personal household, which

increased in number when at the age of six he passed into the company of men. At that stage his instruction began to take the form his father had once known, riding and other such pursuits being prominent among his activities. But he was not as accomplished as his father had been and indeed probably had little interest in sporting activities of any kind. Such was the young prince who, on the death of his father, succeeded to the throne of England, carrying with him all the aspirations of the House of Tudor.

Part Three

Edward VI and Mary I

The Boy King

Where it hath pleased Almighty God, on Friday last past in the morning to call unto his infinite mercy the most excellent high and mighty prince, King Henry VIII of most noble and famous memory, our most dear and entirely beloved father, whose soul God pardon; forasmuch as we, being his only son and undoubted heir, be now invested and established in the crown imperial of this realm, and other his realms, dominions, and countries, with all regalities, pre-eminences, styles, names, titles, and dignities to the same belonging or in any wise appertaining:

We do by these presents signify unto all our said most loving, faithful, and obedient subjects that like as we for our part shall, by God's grace, show ourself a most gracious and benign sovereign lord to all our good subjects in all their just and lawful suits and causes, so we mistrust not but they and every of them will again, for their parts, at all times and in all cases, show themselves unto us,

Thomas, Lord Seymour of Sudeley, brother of the Lord Protector Somerset and Jane Seymour. Although Harding's portrait dates from 1611, its subject died in 1549, having been appointed Lord High Admiral by his brother upon the accession of Edward VI. Following the death of Henry VIII he had married Katherine Parr, and after her death he renewed his earlier attentions to the Princess Elizabeth, though they were repulsed. Committed to the Tower, he was beheaded on March 10, 1549.

their natural liege lord, most faithful, loving, and obedient subjects, according to their bounden duties and allegiances, whereby they shall please God and do the thing that shall tend to their own preservations and sureties; . . .

(Proclamation of the accession of Edward VI, Westminster, January 31, 1547).

Edward VI came to the throne at the age of nine. Although fully aware of his power and inheritance he was clearly incapable of supervising the government of England by himself. Men of affairs who had surrounded Henry VIII jostled for the position of his protector, and ultimately the office went to the warlike Hertford, who promptly created himself Duke of Somerset. In the autumn of 1549 he was usurped from office by Warwick and thrown into the Tower, only to be released the following February. For a while thereafter he and Warwick were on friendly terms, at any rate on the surface; but Warwick gradually assumed the more decisive sway over King Edward, and when he was created Duke of Northumberland during the latter part of 1551 Somerset was sent to the Tower once again, to await execution the following January.

Edward was a dying child, his health worsening all the time. Northumberland therefore assumed a greater power than ever; taking it for granted that his monarch would soon die, he began to seek means whereby the two Tudor princesses could be deprived of their right of succession in favour of Lady Jane Grey, who, as has been mentioned, was the grand-daughter of Henry VIII's sister Mary. For just a brief period of days Northumberland was to have his way, but despite his efforts the Tudor line prevailed.

During his short reign Edward experienced a good deal of unstability. His father had betrothed him to his young cousin, Mary of Scotland, but on July 19, 1551, at the instigation of Northumberland, this match was broken and a treaty signed at Angers betrothing him to the Princess Elizabeth of France. Since Northumberland was fully aware of Edward's precarious physical condition he can only have looked upon this as a temporary diplomatic move, a measure of appeasement to a now relatively strong France on the part of a gravely weakened England. Henry II of France stood in an enviable position, and in acknowledgement of this Northumberland arranged for him to be invested with the Order of the Garter; in return the young English king received the insignia of the Order of St. Michael.

Earlier on in his reign, while Somerset still held sway, Edward had witnessed the remarriage of his step-mother Katherine Parr to Sir Thomas Seymour, brother not only of Jane Seymour but also of the Duke of Somerset. When Katherine died this same Thomas Seymour actually considered a match between himself and the Princess Elizabeth; he also attempted to negotiate a match between Edward and Lady Jane Grey — though this was superseded by the French betrothal. For his scheming and his over-obvious ambition Thomas found himself in the Tower and was beheaded on March 20, 1549. That Somerset was willing to let his own brother go to the scaffold without trial understandably sickened many political observers of the day.

Following Somerset's own execution Northumberland assumed almost total control of the realm, vastly enriching himself in the process. King Edward enjoyed virtually no power, being reduced to compiling a 'Journal' of events that took place outside his jurisdiction. A regular procession to the scaffold was maintained, while the new protector's friends and allies were rewarded with sinecures and titles.

This was a far cry from the early days of Edward's reign, for then he had possessed some slight authority. His coronation took place on February 20, 1547 and thereafter he took an active interest in the political affairs of England,

1555

AET. 74

M. HVGH LATIMER
BISHOP OF WORST.

Latimer preaching before Edward VI at Westminster.

showing a remarkable grasp of the intricacies of government — though he could not have been expected to fathom the full ambitiousness of some of his ministers. He observed also the gradual assumption of executive power by parliament, which before that time had existed mainly as an advisory body. It was the council though that was the principal organ of government during Somerset's time; and in August, 1551 Edward himself was introduced to this body. Once a member, he took an exceedingly active part in the council's proceedings, going so far as to devise a new structure for it. In 1552 he divided its forty members into five committees, each with its separate function, one of them 'for the state', which certain commentators have taken to be the origins of the modern cabinet. Unfortunately Edward's ideas never came to practical fruition.

For many reasons, but mainly because there was no strong arm of government at the time, the country being in the grip of self-seeking ministers, the English economy during the 'boy king's' reign was disappointing. Disgruntlement and even open revolt occurred as a result. Overseas mercantilism however showed distinct success during this period; exploration also was given every encouragement, in part because of the young king's interest in such speculations. At the behest of king and council Sebastian Cabot was enabled to form a company of Merchant Adventurers whose aim it was to discover a north-east passage. By 1553, the last year of Edward's reign, a fleet of three ships set sail under the command of Sir Hugh Willoughby and Richard Chancellor. Two of these craft perished, but Chancellor sailed on as far as Russia, journeyed inland to Moscow and made important arrangements towards the Anglo-Russian trade which was to flourish during the reign of Elizabeth I. After Chancellor's

opposite:
Hugh Latimer, painted by an unknown artist.

99

Aº · 1533 · &
SVÆ ÆTATIS · Z

return in 1555 a so-called Russia Company was formed in London, Cabot being elected its first governor.

Religious issues too occupied Edward and his ministers. The reformation inaugurated by Edward's father was carried a stage further. Religious images and relics were hotly denounced and the English language became rapidly more widespread in church services. During the life of the parliament which met in November, 1547 several notable acts were passed aimed at completely reforming the English Church. Numerous stipulations regarding worship and the position of the Church were made, while Archbishop Latimer preached eloquently in support of the continuing reformation. Finally, in 1549, the Act of Uniformity (discussed elsewhere) was passed.

Apart from his familiar title of the 'boy king', Edward VI is principally remembered as the founder of grammar schools although in fact most of the schools founded during his reign were endowed by private citizens, and indeed most of the schools he himself is averred to have founded existed before his time and merely succeeded in not being closed down by his ministers. Edward died on July 6, 1553 at Greenwich Palace. He had no conception of the turmoil that would follow his death. Like his father's brother, Prince Albert, he died of consumption.

Somerset and Northumberland, Lords Protector

The King's Majesty straightly chargeth and commandeth all his loving subjects with all haste to repair to his highness at his majesty's manor of Hampton Court, in most defensible array, with harness and weapons, to defend his most royal person, and his most entirely beloved uncle the Lord Protector, against whom certain hath attempted a most dangerous conspiracy; and this to do in all possible haste.

(Proclamation of Edward VI, Hampton Court, October 1, 1549).

The Lord Protector Somerset, although he was eventually overthrown by Warwick, stands in the same company of scheming statesmen and courtiers as Wolsey and Cromwell, and later William Cecil; he is one of the most fascinating characters in English history. Brother of Jane Seymour and therefore uncle to Edward VI, he of course had a quite justifiable claim to be recognised as Lord Protector following the death of Henry VIII, and indeed it was this close relationship which finally secured him the position.

Somerset's career of self-advancement had begun with the marriage of his sister Jane Seymour to the second Tudor monarch. At this juncture he had been created Viscount Beauchamp. Four years later, in 1540, he was created Earl of Hertford and a Knight of the Garter. In 1542 he became Lord Chancellor and two years later Lord Lieutenant of the North, conducting the expedition against Scotland mentioned in an earlier section of this publication. By Henry VIII's will Hertford was appointed one of the king's executors and governor of his son Edward; as soon as the processes of intrigue allowed, the Earl of Hertford proclaimed himself Lord Protector of the kingdom, Lord Treasurer, Duke of Somerset and, in 1548, Earl Marshal.

One of Somerset's earliest actions as Protector was to launch a fresh invasion against Scotland. In this he was successful, though all he actually accomplished in the final analysis was an even closer relationship between Scotland and France, Mary, Queen of Scots, being betrothed to the French Dauphin. English and Scottish differences continued until the autumn of 1549, when the English finally withdrew from the northern kingdom (though border skirmishes continued as before), Somerset having declared war against France. This latter issue was finally resolved by the Peace of Boulogne, signed on March 29, 1550, whereby England agreed to cede Boulogne to France (the treaty between England and France of 1546 had actually stipulated 1554 as the date for this transaction), England receiving only 400,000 crowns in compensation. Perhaps of more serious consequence, owing to England's withdrawal from Scotland (a term of the treaty), was that there now existed a very real danger of the latter becoming a French province, a fear much increased by the Dauphin's betrothal to Mary of Scotland.

By this action Somerset reduced England to the rank of a second-rate European power, undoing all that Henry VIII had accomplished. This was not however the direct cause of his downfall; rather it was the unbounded ambition of his rival Warwick.

John Dudley, Earl of Warwick, overthrew and imprisoned Somerset in 1549, even before the Peace of Boulogne had come into effect and while England and France were still at odds, though Somerset was released from the Tower in February, 1550. It was during the ensuing eighteen months that England witnessed one of the most peculiar periods of government that she had ever known, with the two rivals attempting to maintain a status quo jointly, while at the same time trying to prevent themselves coming to blows. Even so, in October, 1551 Warwick was raised to the Dukedom of Northumberland and Somerset was once again sent to the Tower, being finally executed on January 22, 1552. Thereafter Northumberland assumed complete control over the realm. But for the death of Edward the following year he too would undoubtedly have survived to exercise power as completely as Wolsey and Cromwell had done.

Somerset's initial period of power should not be regarded as one of undivided tyranny. He instituted a number of reforms, and his eventual downfall rested upon his disagreement with Warwick over general policy matters, particularly with regard to France. When Warwick became Duke of Northumberland and many of his allies received like elevations — Henry Grey, Marquess of Dorset, became Duke of Suffolk for instance — he both gained the friendship of Edward and so managed the court that it consisted in the main of members of his own faction. It was at this point that he felt himself in a strong enough position to overthrow Somerset once and for all. On a trumped-up charge of conspiracy, backed up by very little evidence, the latter was arrested on October 16, 1551. On December 1 the old Lord Protector was condemned for 'felony'. His execution was delayed, and then arranged with great speed once it was known that parliament would meet on January 23, 1552, when certain of its members might have been expected to speak up in defence of the condemned Somerset. Following Somerset's execution several others suffered the same fate, Northumberland making what amounted to a clean sweep of ministerial offices in order to secure full control of the reins of power.

The story of Northumberland's intriguing to obtain the throne for Lady Jane Grey is dealt with in an appropriate section. He failed in this endeavour, but not without making a considerable mark upon the history of his own times. Jane Grey was proclaimed queen for a while, but the Princess Mary was determined to claim the throne she believed was rightfully hers. Following Jane's fall and Mary's accession Northumberland attempted briefly to reverse his loyalties but he was taken to the Tower.

John Dudley, Duke of Northumberland, who succeeded the Lord Protector Somerset as the most powerful man in England.

The Act of Uniformity and the First Prayer Book

The King's Majesty, by the advice of his most dear uncle, the Lord Protector, and other his highness' council, straightly chargeth and commandeth that no manner person shall sell this present book unbound above the price of 2s. 2d., and bound in forel for 2s. 10d., and not above; and the same bound in sheep's leather for 3s. 3d. and not above; and the same bound in paste or in boards in calves' leather, not above the price of 4s. the piece.

(Proclamation of Edward VI, London, June, 1549).

Archbishop Gardiner was sent to the Tower at the end of June, 1548 for his opposition to the notion of liberalising Church practices in England. At his exit the way was clear for the preparation of a new prayer book for use by Protestants throughout the realm. Released from prison later, Gardiner did give his approval to the new venture, and during the life of the parliament which met between November, 1548 and March, 1549 the first Act of Uniformity was passed, almost all the bishops in the House of Lords supporting it and only three lay peers opposing. The new prayer book, although never approved formally by Convocation, was certainly acceptable to a large number of senior theologians of the time.

This prayer book was the work of Cranmer, a work of great significance in the cultural history of England. Its use in churches was supported by a law stipulating that it and no other should be employed for services. Penalties were fixed according to seriousness of offence and number of offences committed, but although the ultimate penalty for disobedience was life imprisonment they were not savage for the age in which they were conceived, an age in which 'heretics' could be burnt at the stake on the flimsiest pretence. Laymen were permitted to absent themselves from the new service and pass unpunished, but even for those who expressed open contempt for its form the penalty on a first conviction was limited to a fine of £10.

The Act of Uniformity was the culmination of Henry VIII's severance from Rome and the establishment of royal supremacy. Edward VI's accession while still in his minority created certain problems in this respect and many held that royal supremacy could not in fact be proclaimed until the new monarch had attained his majority (at the age of 24). In favour of this argument was the fact that whereas Henry VIII had held absolute power throughout the realm in all matters of government, his young son could lay no claim at all to this circumstance. The youth's premature death arrested all debate on this problem for the time being.

In compiling the new prayer book Cranmer was obliged to make concessions to many people in England who, despite Henry VIII's actions, still owed allegiance to Rome. Adherents of the new Zwinglian denomination in England, which heatedly opposed the Vatican, were greatly upset by this fact; however, when the new prayer book was considered for formal approval by parliament various other matters respecting the status and activities of priests were also regulated, and among several changes was the approval of the marriage of priests.

The neat script of Thomas Cranmer, in 1537.

Edward VI's coronation medal, struck by Henry Basse.

Naturally opposition to the new order was by no means universally passive in character, especially among the laity. Fully Englished church services caused considerable offence, markedly in the west country; men and women felt that their religious devotions were being somehow debased, simplified to the point of being almost commonplace. Opposition came also from academic clerics, as well as papal sympathisers, so that ultimately Cranmer perceived that his aim of total reform was virtually untenable. During the two years following the first Act of Uniformity he was obliged to consider terms for a second Act and the composition of a second prayer book.

Cranmer produced a revised prayer book in 1551; this was finally authorised by parliament the following year, Edward VI himself having earlier threatened to make improvements to the litany. The revised communion service still contained references to the flesh and blood of Christ and communicants were still required to kneel during the service, which latter caused bitter friction among certain reforming clerics and their opponents. John Knox, who had introduced the sitting posture in his communion services, was one particularly noteworthy enemy of kneeling, and in September, 1552 he went so far as to preach angrily upon the matter before the king himself. Edward was so affected by Knox's language that he requested Cranmer, Ridley and their allies to think again over this question. They did so, but opted finally in favour of the kneeling posture; however, as a result of Knox's vehemence when the new prayer book finally saw the light of day it included the notorious 'Black Rubric', which simply recorded that kneeling was intended to express mere devotion, not adoration. Various other simplifications were incorporated in this second prayer book. The second Act of Uniformity differed from the first in providing strict penalties for clergy who employed any other form of service, and stipulated that the laity who did not attend services were liable to punishment, especially if they attended any unauthorised form of service instead.

To conclude the matter of establishing a new form of public worship revised Articles of Faith were written, again prepared under the direction of Cranmer. They were 42 in number (although Cranmer is said to have written down a total of 54, the other twelve presumably being overruled by his bishops). During the reign of Elizabeth I these were to be superseded by the 39 Articles. Prominent among the tenets of Cranmer's Articles was the assumption that the King of England was supreme head of the Church of England and Ireland, answerable only to Christ.

Cranmer's dogmatism, like Gardiner's stubbornness, would eventually tell against him. His achievement was however significant, for it saw the completion of the process begun by Henry VIII.

opposite:
Archbishop Cranmer.

Discontent and risings
in the provinces

... his Majesty ... hath thought it meet to signify unto all and singular his loving subjects that if they or any of them shall know any manner of conspiracy or other privy intent of insurrection or rising to be made, moved, or attempted, by any person or persons within any shire, place, or places of this his said realm (and before open knowledge thereof had) do with all expedition make the same to be known, either to his highness or unto his Privy Council or unto his majesty's lieutenant of the county and shire where any such thing shall be intended, moved, or determined, and the same accusation, by any mean lawfully or duly proved, shall not only have of the king's majesty, for his pains and labor, for every such matter or privy intent so disclosed and proved (as is aforesaid), although he or they be one of the conspiracy, the sum of £20, but also his majesty's benign favor and pardon, with thanks for the same accordingly.

(Proclamation of Edward VI, Greenwich, May 17, 1550).

Throughout the Tudor era rulers had been obliged to contend with a high incidence of provincial unrest. The short reign of Edward VI provided no exception; nor were religious factors the only causes of discontent in his time. Even so, a revolt in the west country during June, 1549 arose entirely from the publication of the first English prayer book. Exeter withstood a siege of some six weeks duration, being relieved on August 6 by Russell, assisted by mercenaries from as far afield as Italy and Germany. It required a further eleven days for the rebels to be dispelled altogether.

Other risings occurred in Oxfordshire, where demonstrating priests caught by Grey were actually hanged from their own church steeples. However, the most significant of all risings during this period was that in Norfolk which had economic and agrarian rather than purely religious causes. A somewhat isolated group of people, Norfolk farmers had not taken kindly to the recent imposition of land enclosure, the instigation of manorial rights and other enforcements. Slight unrest had been apparent here from the very beginning of Edward's reign, but when it became clear to the populace that the Lord Protector himself was against the enclosure of land, and when on June 14, 1549 he issued a proclamation to the effect that those who had pulled down the offending enclosures would be pardoned, he gave impetus to the men of Norfolk to air their grievances once and for all.

During the second week in July a noisy meeting of Norfolk men at Wymondham fell beneath the sway of one Robert Kett, a local tanner and landowner. His action in removing the fences placed around his own land had commanded much local admiration; his angry oratory quickly attracted popular support from all parts of Norfolk, and even from parts of Suffolk. Between July 12 and August 26, 1549, together with a force of some 12,000 rebels, he succeeded in maintaining control over Norwich from a camp established on nearby Mousehold Heath.

Kett's rebellion was characterised by a complete lack of violence, he and his followers satisfying themselves with the simple demand 'that all bondmen be made free'. Their demands were duly ignored, but royal pardons were proposed (the 'rebels' probably did not consider themselves to be such — violence being

Detail from the title page of the Illustrium Majoris Britanniae *of John Bale, published in 1548. Bale's writings were denounced by Mary I.*

excluded from their actions — but the law nevertheless classified them in this way). The continued opposition of these Norfolk men and the increase in their degree of organisation at last caused concern at court. Their destruction was finally ordained, the Marquess of Northampton (formerly Sir William Parr) leading the expedition.

Northampton took Norwich on July 30, 1549. He was expelled again within a very short time, and it was only on August 23 that troops under Warwick himself approached the city. Four days later Kett and his followers moved from their camp and made for Dunindale nearby. During the move he was attacked by the king's forces and lost altogether 3,000 men. During December, following the collapse of his supporters, Kett and his clerical brother were both condemned to death for treason. Kett was hanged at Norwich castle, his brother from the church steeple at Wymondham.

As an expression of local discontent this rebellion was notable, though on a wider plane it had little effect. As far as the government of England was concerned, one of its main outcomes was to abet Warwick's rise and the consequent lowering of Somerset's fortunes.

Lady Jane Grey

Treason doth never prosper: what's the reason?
For if it prosper, none dare call it treason.

(Sir John Harington, 1561-1612).

The ten days reign of Lady Jane Grey presents one of the most curious incidents in all of English history. Her proposed accession was wholly untenable from the outset and was entirely the scheme of Northumberland, who hoped by her elevation to increase his own hold on the realm. Her fate was cruel, but in the climate of her times only to be expected. With her fall the fall also of Northumberland was assured.

Northumberland's actions can only be described as ill-judged. In early 1553 it had become clear that Edward VI would not live long, and as a result the Lord Protector persuaded the boy to 'devise' his crown to Jane Grey, his seventeen year old cousin once removed and daughter of Frances, Duchess of Suffolk, granddaughter of Henry VIII's sister Mary who had married Charles Brandon, Duke of Suffolk. After Jane's death the crown was to pass into the possession of her male heir.

Why the Princess Mary and Elizabeth were passed over Northumberland did not trouble to explain; nor did he explain why Lady Jane Grey should be offered the throne in preference to her own mother. Northumberland's wishes were in fact entirely based on a desire to keep Mary from the throne; by marrying Jane to his own son, Lord Guildford Dudley, he aimed at ensuring the promulgation of his own authority. That he failed was hardly surprising.

Yet Lady Jane Grey was not at all an unpersonable young lady, and she was renowned both for her beauty and her intelligence. Her father, Henry Grey,

Marquess of Dorset and Duke of Suffolk (1551), was Lord High Constable of England; although he escaped execution at the time of his daughter's fall, being instead imprisoned in the Tower for only a short period, he lost his head in 1554 for taking part in Wyatt's rebellion. His daughter was born in 1537 at Broadgate Hall in Leicestershire, and educated under the tutelage of John Aylmer, Bishop of London. Her learning was remarkable, for in addition to other accomplishments she was fluent in Latin, Greek, French and Italian, as well as knowing something of Hebrew, Chaldean and Arabic.

opposite:
Lady Jane Grey.

Edward having agreed to the device whereby this attractive girl should succeed him, Northumberland set about persuading lawyers to execute a royal will indicating it as a part of Edward's own express desire. Only one legal member of the council — Sir James Hales — demurred, and the desired document was signed by more than a hundred people, including the most powerful in the land. Even Cranmer, who was however the last to sign, declared that he did so without reservation. With the backing of Henry II of France, Northumberland now considered the day was his: though all the French monarch wished to secure was the promotion of his daughter-in-law, Mary Queen of Scots, rather than of Princess Mary of England. Mary Tudor, on the other hand, was determined that Northumberland should not succeed and that she would finally occupy the English throne.

Edward died on June 6, 1553. Northumberland kept the fact of his death unrevealed for three days. On June 10 Jane Grey was brought to London and accommodated in the Tower (which was not exclusively employed for purposes of imprisonment); later that same day she was proclaimed queen. Lord Robert Dudley was despatched to take Mary into custody, but the young princess had already fled, more determined than ever to claim the throne for herself. She had hastily journeyed to Norfolk and encountered opposition; she found refuge finally at Framlingham and slowly acquired a vigorous body of supporters. Spurred by their numbers, on June 9 she despatched a letter to the council demanding that she be proclaimed queen (the letter was received two days later).

Northumberland naturally dismissed this request, but he failed to bargain for public opinion which at this point turned against him. His present manner of abusing his power had led to very real fears for his conduct once he assumed complete control over the occupant of the throne; nor could the possibility be ruled out of his own son assuming kingship in the event of Jane Grey's death. Although he did not personally approve the move, Northumberland's next action was to leave London at the head of a troop of 3,000 horse, a number of foot soldiers and some thirty guns in order to confront Mary and her followers.

Even as Northumberland marched out against her, Mary was being proclaimed queen in several of the southern counties; worrying news accompanied these tidings in the form of intelligence that certain one-time supporters of Northumberland had switched their allegiance to Mary. Taking refuge at Cambridge, on June 20 the Lord Protector conceded that his cause was now futile. There he attempted to display a reversal of his loyalties by suddenly proclaiming Mary the rightful queen, but he must have known that his action would not be taken seriously.

Mary was acclaimed with great enthusiasm in London, and those who had at first opposed her succession hurried to fend for themselves as best they could — some, like William Cecil, quite truthfully affirming that they signed the terms of Edward VI's will against their better judgement. Numerous offenders went to the Tower: Northumberland, Suffolk, Lord Robert Dudley and many others.

Mary entered London on August 3, 1553 in the company of her sister, the Princess Elizabeth. One of her earliest actions was to pardon certain men and women then being held in captivity, including Bishop Gardiner; however, as her ensuing reign was to demonstrate again and again, she showed little mercy

Mary I and her reign

We do signify unto you that according to our said right and title we do take upon us and be in the just and lawful possession of the same; not doubting but that all our true and faithful subjects will so accept us, take us, and obey us as their natural and liege sovereign lady and Queen, according to the duties of their allegiance; assuring all our good and faithful subjects that in their so doing they shall find us their benign and gracious sovereign lady, as others our most noble progenitors have heretofore been.

(Announcement of the accession of Mary I. *'Queen of England, France, and Ireland, defender of the faith, and in the earth supreme head of the Church of England and Ireland'*, London, July 19, 1553).

Mary's short reign of five years duration began with her entry into London on August 3, 1553. It was by no means the domestically peaceful reign that might have been expected, for it embraced the restoration of Roman Catholicism and the numerous burnings at the stake consequent upon that action. In many ways Mary's reign can be looked upon as but a prelude to the reign of her half-sister Elizabeth, but it is by no means without interest. Of particular importance in her own day was the fact that Mary was a mature woman, born on February 8, 1516 and some 37 years of age at the time of her accession. This was a far cry from the reign of the late 'boy king' her brother.

Naturally the coming of a new monarch meant a reshuffle among ministers and other high officials. With the marriage of Mary to the future Philip II of Spain in 1554 it also meant a certain realignment of foreign interests. Before this latter event took place parliament decreed that the authority of the English monarch must remain unchanged following the queen's marriage and that Philip should take no part in the government of England. If their marriage proved childless and Mary should die first Philip should retain no interest at all in England.

During the early part of her reign Mary's principal concern was to reconcile England with Rome. Her marriage to the Catholic King of Naples and Jerusalem (as Philip had been styled by his father) was naturally seen as a first move in this direction. Her refusal to take English opinion on the matter into account, which naturally caused rebellion, was a firm indication of her strong-willed personality.

Although Philip's interest in the English throne was intended to be minimal, and despite the fact that any male issue of his and Mary's union might conceivably have a claim on the Spanish throne in the future, Englishmen at large opposed the marriage. Sir Thomas Wyatt, son of the poet of that name,

'wherfore y shall moste earnestly requyre you (the premysses consydered) to thynke non vnkyndnes in me, thoughe y refuse to be a medler any wayes in thys matter, assuryng you, that (womeny matters set aparte, wherin y beeng a mayde am nothyng comyng) if other wayes it shall lye in my litle power to do you playser, y shalbe as gladde to do it, as you to requyre it / both for hys Bloddy sake, that you be of, and also for the gentylnes, whiche y have alwayes founde in you. As knoweth almygty god to whose tuicyon y comytte you from waltyed thys saterday at nygt beeng the vij^th of june

your assured frend to my powey Marye /

took the lead in the resultant rebellion that still bears his name, relishing the opportunity it gave him to indulge in madcap enterprise. He intended to overthrow the queen; while his own approaches to the Princess Elizabeth perhaps suggested that he had other motives as well. He recruited his followers in Kent, arranging for other dissatisfied gentlemen to follow suit in other parts of the kingdom. Matters did not finally proceed as Wyatt intended; nevertheless, towards the end of January, 1554 he was able to march on London at the head of 4,000 men. The Duke of Norfolk, despatched originally to thwart him, transferred his allegiance to Wyatt, but when the rebel gained Southwark and London Bridge on February 3 he found to his dismay that London was already armed in readiness against him. The queen had personally succeeded in persuading the populace to oppose the rebel. On February 6 Wyatt ostensibly retreated, only to march westwards to Kingston, cross the Thames there and approach London via Knightsbridge. On February 7 he withstood opposition near what is today Hyde Park Corner and proceeded to Fleet Street. There his ambitions came to an abrupt conclusion, for he could not penetrate Ludgate, nor were there means of retreat. He surrendered without giving battle and was conveyed to the Tower that same day. Forty six rebels were hanged and Wyatt himself was beheaded on April 11.

It was in the wake of this affair that Lady Jane Grey and her husband were beheaded, on February 12, although they had played no part in Wyatt's uprising. Both Northumberland and his brother Lord Thomas Grey followed them in due course. It was also following these troubles that the Princess Elizabeth incurred her half-sister's enmity, being imprisoned in the Tower on March 18, 1554 and fully expecting not to emerge alive. It was shown that she had indeed corresponded with the disgraced Wyatt, but there was otherwise no evidence of her having been implicated in the traitor's action. Before his death Wyatt publicly disclaimed any intrigue on Elizabeth's part; she was released from custody on May 19 and hurried off to Woodstock where she remained for several months.

As her chancellor, Mary appointed the Bishop of Winchester, Stephen Gardiner, who had offered such opposition to Cranmer at the time of the latter's compiling the English prayer book. Gardiner held the office for two years, and in retrospect can be seen as one of the most remarkable men of his time. He died on November 12, 1555 and with his passing Mary lost her firmest arm of government. Much savagery was perpetrated during this reign, and if Gardiner did not give it his approval he at any rate made no serious attempt to put an end to it. He was succeeded by Nicholas Heath, created Archbishop of York in the same year. Heath was not strong in office, and for the remainder of Mary's reign he was partly overshadowed by his superior, the papal legate and Archbishop of Canterbury, Cardinal Pole.

Reginald Pole was born in 1500. He had been forced to flee the country during Henry VIII's reign, but succeeded Cranmer as Archbishop of Canterbury in 1555. He died on the day of the queen's funeral, November 18, 1558, and indeed it had been the good will of his sovereign which had secured him his high office. Although his position as papal legate entailed the perpetration of much violent recrimination in his name he was not personally of a cruel disposition, indeed, his mildness from time to time earned him the disapproval of his superiors at Rome.

Pole's great determination in office was to stamp out what he took to be the abuses of the clergy, and like his predecessors he undertook the publication of new series of homilies, a revised prayer book and even a new translation of the New Testament. He failed in his attempts to reform the newly established Roman Catholic Church in England mainly because of opposition from Rome itself, specifically from Pope Paul V, elected to office in May, 1555. In June, 1557 the latter deprived Pole of his position and summoned him to Rome to answer charges of heresy, though in fact this never took place.

In the meantime Philip had succeeded to the throne in Spain (1556) on the abdication of his father, and when disagreement subsequently arose over the sovereignty of the Kingdom of Naples Philip had been excommunicated. Quite naturally Mary found herself in uneasy circumstances, not knowing whether to show loyalty to her husband or to Rome. She gave it finally to her husband, in part as a result of the pope's treatment of Pole, her favourite.

During Mary's reign continental troubles plagued England incessantly, and unhappily it was Spain which caused a good deal of the unrest. But perhaps it was the English loss of Calais that most perturbed the ruling faction of the time. On June 7, 1557 England once again declared war on France, this time in support of Spain, who was being menaced by the French for her actions in Italy. At first England had been loath to come to Spain's assistance, but finally she

The burial of Queen Mary, taken from Holinshed's Chronicles. *(Not intended as a realistic record of the event, this illustration was used several times throughout Holinshed's work, in connection with different people).*

113

H

agreed and during July some 4,000 troops under the command of Pembroke crossed the Channel. The joint English and Spanish army at first enjoyed complete success and Paris was soon at its mercy, a major victory being scored on August 10 at St. Quentin.

Circumstances altered rapidly. The English garrison at Calais was attacked by the French on January 1, 1558 and a week later Lord Wentworth, the commander, surrendered. The English council had seriously underestimated the French threat in this quarter, and, certainly not expecting a winter attack, had withdrawn its fleet from the area. The loss of Calais, which had been an English possession for more than two centuries, was followed on January 20 by Lord Grey of Wilton's surrender of Guisnes. To England the loss of Calais was on the face of it extremely serious, though subsequent events were to demonstrate that possession of the French port was not so essential to English trading interests as had always been assumed. Mary herself is supposed to have averred (though there is no substantiation for it): 'When I am dead and opened, you shall find "Calais" lying in my heart'.

Fighting with France continued in the Low Countries, but mainly at the instigation of Philip II who could now be quite plainly seen as taking advantage of his English connection for Spanish ends. The war ended only in July, 1558, though a treaty was not concluded at Cateau-Cambrésis until April, 1559, after Mary's death.

Mary died on November 17, 1558. To the last she continued her endeavours to restore Roman Catholicism. She did not produce an heir, though she had long hoped for one, and she was reconciled during her last days to her half-sister Elizabeth inheriting the crown (and it was openly thought that when her death became imminent Philip actually made overtures to the Princess Elizabeth).

opposite:
Philip II of Spain.

Philip II of Spain

First, it is covenanted and agreed, etc., that as soon as conveniently may be, a true, pure, and perfect marriage shall by words of the present tense be contracted, celebrated, and consummated between the foresaid noble Prince and most noble lady the Queen in their proper persons in England; by virtue of which marriage so contracted, celebrated, and consummated, the said most noble Prince Philip shall for so long as the matrimony endureth be allowed to have and enjoy jointly together with the same most noble Queen his wife the style, honor, and kingly name of the realms and dominions unto the same most noble Queen appertaining, and shall aid the same most noble Queen his wife in the prosperous administration of her realms and dominions; saving neverthe-less the rights, laws, privileges, and customs of the same realms and dominions.

(Article of the marriage between Mary I and Philip of Spain, dated Westminster, January 14, 1554).

That the King of Spain and the Queen of England should become husband and wife did not seem incongruous at a time when international match-making among royal families was a recognised practice. It did, however, lead to a certain amount of unrest and as was to be expected with Spain having numerous problems of her own, Philip was frequently separated from his wife.

Philip was the son of the Emperor Charles V of Germany and Isabella of Portugal, born on May 21, 1527 (Charles' mother Juana was the daughter of Ferdinand and Isabella of Spain, and by this connection he became King of Spain in 1516, under the title of Charles I; he was elected Emperor of Germany in 1519 on the death of Maximilian I, his father Philip having been the Archduke of Austria). Philip's succession to the Spanish throne took place following his father's abdication in 1556. He married Mary I of England in 1554, and from then until her death in 1558 ruled jointly with his wife as King of England but renouncing all claim to the English throne at her death. In 1580 when the direct male line of the Portuguese royal family became extinct he claimed that throne also, annexing it to Spain. He died in the Escurial at Madrid on September 13, 1598, by which time he had lived to see the English navy defeat his own Armada in 1588.

Philip and Mary were in fact cousins, a papal dispensation allowing their wedding to take place (though this dispensation was in itself no longer valid in English law). Their marriage, on July 25, 1554, was solemnised by Bishop Gardiner in Winchester Cathedral. All splendour and pageantry attended this ceremony, and it was followed by a stately progress towards London, which Philip and Mary entered on August 18. To Mary, marriage to a Catholic prince was all a part of her policy of restoring Roman Catholicism in England; however, the twenty waggons full of gold from Spain that accompanied the royal pair to London following their marriage at Winchester indicated one further very strong inducement.

Mary was not Philip's first wife, for he had previously married Maria, the daughter of John III of Portugal, in 1543. Following Mary's death, in 1560 he married Isabella of Valois, daughter of Henry II of France. Lastly he married Anne, daughter of the Emperor Maximilian II of Germany, in 1570. Philip's matrimonial dealings were all of a political nature, and as can be seen from this tally the man who had been fighting the French in 1558 married the King of France's daughter two years later; and similarly the man who jointly occupied the throne of England for four years and who had begged the support of English arms in his own cause was in 1588 to launch an attack on England.

The return to Rome

Her highness therefore straightly chargeth and commandeth all and every of her subjects, of whatsoever state, condition, or degree they be, that none of them presume henceforth to preach, or by way of reading in churches or other public or private places (except in the schools of the universities) to interpret or teach any Scriptures or any manner points of doctrine concerning religion;

neither also to print any books, matter, ballad, rhyme, interlude, process, or treatise, nor to play any interlude save they have her grace's special license in writing for the same; upon pain to incur her highness' indignation and displeasure.

(Proclamation of Mary I, August 18, 1553).

A Mary I 'royal' of 1553, now preserved in the British Museum and the only known example of this date. The obverse is shown here, much enlarged.

It was on November 30, 1554 that England became fully reconciled with Rome. The process by which this swift about-turn of English religious affairs was achieved dated from August the previous year when commissions were issued for the enquiry into those sees where irregularities were said to have taken place. As a result many one-time Roman Catholic bishops were restored to their sees. At the same time it was decreed that all religious changes instituted during the reign of Edward VI were to be reversed.

At this early stage of the queen's reign no mention was made of Rome, and Mary's supremacy as head of the English Church was assumed to be still as decreed by her father, Henry VIII. She persevered however, and during March, 1554 two further commissions were issued depriving seven more Protestant bishops of their sees, in most instances on the grounds that they had married. Certain other bishops had in any case already resigned in anticipation, and with the fall of Cranmer the Archbishopric of Canterbury had also become vacant. During the same month injunctions were issued whereby the bishops were to rout out additionally all those among their clerics who had in any way offended against Mary's new tenets. By this means something like a fifth of the clergy in England at the time were removed from their benefices (possibly as many as 1,500 priests).

The next stage in Mary's reforms incorporated her marriage to Philip, approved by parliament during the session beginning April 2, 1554. In the meantime such men as Cranmer, Latimer and Ridley were held in captivity awaiting their trials for heresy and final execution, each of them being invited, but each of them refusing, to recant (although Cranmer did recant finally, only to withdraw his recantations when he realised that his action was futile). Many others were treated likewise. Following her marriage Mary personally directed her council to request the Vatican to send her a papal legate. The legate appointed was Reginald Pole, who carried out a visitation of English churches and by his presence succeeded in giving authority to the burning of heretics in London. Mary herself did not look upon these executions as acts of cruelty, but rather of purification, as examples to the greater mass of citizens.

Pole arrived in England during the autumn of 1554. Although he had been powerful during the early part of Henry VIII's reign and had amassed considerable riches (he still drew benefices from parishes he had never visited), he had been obliged to flee the country following the separation from Rome. He had remained safely abroad during the remainder of Henry VIII's lifetime and during the reign of Edward VI, and now he was a full cardinal enjoying the favour of the Vatican. Reginald Pole possessed one other great advantage, for he was himself of royal descent, being brother of Henry Pole, Lord Montague, and son of Margaret, Countess of Salisbury (herself executed in 1541) and daughter of George, Duke of Clarence, the brother of Edward IV and Richard III. By the time Pole arrived in England the surviving Catholic bishops had all been restored to their sees.

Philip's gold had assisted in the restoration of these bishops, and now all that was required was for England formally to reconcile herself with Rome. On November 29 parliament approved a petition to be received once again into the Catholic Church, only two members of the House of Commons opposing this petition and none from the House of Lords. The day following England was absolved of her schismatic offence, being embraced once more by Rome.

Following this transaction a good deal of legislation became necessary: old heresy laws were revived and all bills passed against the authority of Rome since the time of Henry VIII were replaced. Monastic lands and titles were not however restored to the Church, as Pole had clearly hoped they would be. Thus the will of Mary's father in one respect at any rate was observed.

Latimer, Ridley and others burnt at the stake

The King and Queen our sovereign lord and lady therefore (most entirely and earnestly tendering the preservation and safety, as well of the souls as of the bodies, lands, and substance of all their good and loving subjects and others, and minding to root out and extinguish all false doctrine and heresies and other occasions of schisms, divisions, and sects that come by the same heresies and false doctrine) straightly charge and command that no person or persons, of what estate, degree, or condition soever he or they be, from henceforth presume to bring or convey or cause to be brought or conveyed into this realm any books, writings, or works hereafter mentioned:

That is to say, any book or books, writings or works made or set forth by or in the name of Martin Luther, or any book or books, writings or works made or set forth by or in the name of Oecolampadius, Zwinglius, John Calvin, Pemeraine, John Alasco, Bullinger, Bucer, Melancthon, Bernardinus Ochinus, Erasmus Sarcerius, Peter Martyr, Hugh Latimer, Robert Barnes, otherwise called Friar Barnes, John Bale, otherwise called Friar Bale, Justus Jonas, John Hooper, Miles Coverdale, William Tyndale, Thomas Cranmer, late Archbishop of Canterbury, William Turner, Theodore Basille, otherwise called Thomas Becon, John Frith, Roy, and the book commonly called Hall's Chronicles, *or any of them, in the Latin tongue, Dutch tongue, English tongue, Italian tongue, or French tongue, or any other like book, paper, writing, or work made, printed, or set forth by any other person or persons, containing false doctrine contrary and against the Catholic faith and the doctrine of the Catholic church; . . .*

(Proclamation of Mary I, against heresy, Hampton Court, June 13, 1555).

Mary's reign was characterised by fierce reprisals against those who did not favour the return to Rome. Heretics were burnt, and their heresy was assessed not by a secular but by a clerical court. However, not even the Church could actually ordain a burning, and royal approval had to be secured for each heretical conviction. Thus although Pole was active in the persecution of heretics it was Mary herself who took the final decision to approve their sentences (Stephen Gardiner, who gave tacit approval to the new policy, did not himself condemn any heretics). The list of those who died at the stake gradually assumed dramatic proportions.

The harsh policy did not yield altogether the required results. All of those who died at the stake initially did so bravely, many of them martyrs who were offered their lives in exchange for recantation but who refused. The trials began

towards the end of January, 1555 and within a very few days, under the direction of Edmund Bonner, Bishop of London and a zealous pursuer of heretics, the first martyrs went to their deaths: Hooper, Ferrar, Rowland Taylor, Saunders, John Rogers (the latter the editor of Tyndale's translation of the New Testament). The general public by and large was outraged, and for a brief while those intent on carrying out the burnings were worried, though they quickly resumed their activities.

Two major trials took place during the autumn of 1555, when on September 30 and October 1 Ridley and Latimer stood trial at Oxford. Both were condemned; both, on account of their having been neither monks nor married, could have recanted and been pardoned, but neither did and they were burnt on October 16. Latimer observed to his fellow sufferer on this occasion: 'We shall this day light such a candle, by God's grace, in England as shall never be put out'. His words have endured and still retain their force.

Archbishop Cranmer too faced this barbarous rite. His punishment was savagely prolonged, first of all by his case being referred to Rome, where he was ultimately burnt in effigy, and then by Rome referring it back to the English courts. The queen signed the order for his execution on February 24, 1556, but although many of Cranmer's predecessors at the stake had been burnt forthwith he was kept waiting a full month before his sentence was carried out. Although his enemies had no intention of pardoning him they endeavoured throughout this period to extract a recantation from him, which they knew could well prove to be a most valuable document. They succeeded: for by freeing Cranmer temporarily from the misery of prison, and by taking advantage of his slight misgivings about the question of royal supremacy following the death of Henry VIII (a circumstance abolished by the return of papal authority), they did in fact extract four submissions and two recantations from him, which included an admission of his own offences. Having armed themselves with these his detractors promptly set the date of his execution for March 21. Cranmer attempted another recantation on the eve of his death, but to no effect.

To many it might at this point have appeared that Cranmer had given way to cowardice. In fact his attempt to save his own life was no more than a

The martyrdom of Ridley and Latimer, an engraving from a later edition of Foxe's Actes and Monuments.

recognition that by staying alive he could quite possibly accomplish more than by becoming a martyr. When he saw there was no saving himself he withdrew all his recantations and at his death, by the famous remark referred to elsewhere, he triumphed over his persecutors.

Cranmer and other well known church dignitaries provided but a handful of the full complement of 'heretics' who met their deaths at the stake during Mary's reign. A grand total of almost 300 martyrs were committed to the flames; nor were the living alone submitted to this indignity: certain past offenders were actually exhumed and their remains burnt.

The records of Mary's burnings have been preserved for all time in a most remarkable book, the *Actes and Monuments* of John Foxe (normally referred to today as the 'martyrologist', his book being more commonly known as the *Book of Martyrs*), based as far as Foxe was able to do so on contemporary sources and first published in 1563. This book is still frequently referred to today, having passed through several editions over the centuries. Its realistic illustrations and impassioned descriptions cannot even now fail to horrify the reader and lead him to question how such a policy could ever have been carried out in the name of Christian religion.

Part Four

Elizabeth I

The beginning of Elizabeth's reign

Have a care over my people. You have my people — do you that which I ought to do. They are my *people. Every man oppresseth and spoileth them without mercy. They cannot revenge their quarrel, nor help themselves. See unto them — see unto them, for they are my charge. I charge you, even as God hath charged me. I care not for myself; my life is not dear to me. My care is for my people. I pray God, whoever succeedeth me, be as careful of them as I am.*

(Queen Elizabeth I to her judges upon appointing them in 1559).

With the accession to the throne of Mary's sister, Elizabeth I, England entered one of her most glorious eras. Elizabeth succeeded Mary on November 17, 1558, though at the time many observers took it for granted that she would not succeed in retaining the throne for very long and that Mary Stuart of Scotland, then married to the French Dauphin, would put forward a strong claim for the English crown.

Elizabeth arrived in London to assume her new calling on November 23, 1558, her coronation taking place on January 15 the following year. Her entry into the city was a triumph, while the procession that preceded her coronation provided a magnificent spectacle. Pageant upon pageant had been prepared to honour the new queen on this latter occasion, a large number of them embodying themes expressing the high hopes the English nation was placing in its new ruler. Many of them pointed to past injustices and to the expectation that in the future the ills of Mary's reign would be replaced by freedom of thought and justice.

It is of interest to note that this form of public celebration was one of the authentic popular dramatic forms of the early Elizabethan era, employing moving stage carriages of two decks, the upper one containing standard pieces of theatrical scenery such as movable suns and moons as well as providing an upper platform for performers. Throughout her reign, as she made grand progresses about the southern portion of her realm, as well as encouraging more conventional dramatic fare in London, Elizabeth was to be a great patroness of the spectacle, as well as the court masque.

Thus Elizabeth's coming was heralded with almost unanimous rejoicing. The twenty five year old queen, although an unknown entity, was said to be highly learned — which indeed she was — and in addition had already demonstrated a part of her ability to hold her own by avoiding implication in any plots discovered against her predecessor on the throne. Principal among her inherited problems was the religious turmoil which had been inflicted upon the kingdom by Mary; while abroad there was France to contend with, and not far away on the horizon there lay a dangerous adversary in the person of Philip II of Spain.

Elizabeth was fortunate in her choice of Sir William Cecil whom she appointed as Secretary of State after her coronation. Cecil had that eminently satisfactory quality of being able to serve under several masters and yet cause no lasting offence to any. He had already served under both Somerset and Warwick, and even under the rule of Mary had held an important position. In later life he was to acquire great eminence; however, at the time of Elizabeth's accession he was a comparatively insignificant minister. Although Cecil was not to develop into a schemer such as Wolsey or Cromwell his importance to Elizabeth was to be as great as theirs had been to her father.

The religious inheritance was not Elizabeth's sole worry. Since her legitimacy of birth had not been correctly established following her father's rejection of her mother, she was plagued with the circumstance that her claim to the throne was not an authenticated one. But above even that was the pressing insistence of her ministers, led by the Speaker of the House of Commons, Sir Thomas Gargrave, that she should find herself a husband and provide the kingdom with an heir. It was at this juncture that the new queen gave magnificent evidence of her own independence of mind, as well as a hint of how her reign would be conducted in the future. She refused to entertain their suggestion and went so far as to suggest that figuratively speaking she had already become married: to the kingdom of England, all of whose citizens were her children. She wore a special ring to signify this and hinted that she proposed to live and die a virgin queen, and this promise she upheld.

It was not until the end of 1559, on December 17, that Parker was appointed Archbishop of Canterbury, though he did not take on the employment lightly and was not anxious to accept the promotion. The second luminary of the early years of Elizabeth's reign, Parker was born in 1504. At one time he had been chaplain to Anne Boleyn, Elizabeth's mother, becoming in 1557 Dean of Lincoln. During the reign of Mary he had lived in retirement. His legacy to the nation was significant, for in addition to making bequests to Cambridge University he published a new edition of the Bible known as the 'Bishop's Bible' at his own expense and founded the still existing Society of Antiquaries.

Although of a reclusive disposition, more given to the attractions of scholarship than the affairs of state, once the queen and her secretary of state had persuaded him to take up his supreme office he showed himself to be an unexpectedly proficient servant of the realm. His job was a difficult one, the entire body of the clergy being in a condition of disarray and unease and with so many religious reversals having occurred since the time of Henry VIII that few men were able to ascertain with any degree of sureness that the new arrangements would persist.

The third of Elizabeth's early ministers of outstanding ability was Sir Nicholas Bacon, appointed Lord Keeper of the Great Seal in 1558. Father of the more famous Francis Bacon, he was born in 1510 and as a young man had studied law. Appointed to the office of Attorney of the Court of Wards in 1546, he had kept his situation during the reign of Edward VI but been deprived of it by Mary. Under Elizabeth he was restored, knighted, appointed a Privy Councillor and promoted to high office. He temporarily lost patronage of the queen in 1564 when he published a pamphlet about the succession of the crown, but Cecil (by that time Burghley) quickly returned him to his queen's favour. It was of this able statesman, who in later years grew exceedingly fat, that Elizabeth is supposed to have remarked 'Sir Nicholas' soul lodges well'.

Matthew Parker, Archbishop of Canterbury under Elizabeth I until his death in 1575. When upon one occasion the queen paid him a visit she met so many married prelates that she took her leave of Parker's wife with the following words: 'Madam I may not call you; mistress I am ashamed to call you; and so I know not what to call you; but howsoever I thank you'.

Elizabeth's favourites

I am resolved to marry when the necessity of my affairs and the welfare of my subjects require it; but I believe it better to marry a foreigner rather than one of my own kingdom for my honour and grandeur. Nevertheless, if there be no foreigner agreeable to me, nor one who can comply with my conditions, I shall be compelled to marry within my own kingdom; I shall then choose no other than the Earl of Leycester because of the merits and virtues which I know him to possess.

(Elizabeth I to the French Ambassador, 1556).

Throughout her reign Elizabeth had many 'favourites' who enjoyed considerable patronage and influence at court. It is customary to believe that some of them were suitors to the queen and that upon occasion their attentions were not at all ill received. Elizabeth however never married, and posterity may now decide at its will just what relationship Elizabeth enjoyed with certain of her courtiers. The names of Leicester and Essex have passed down into history, and much of their glamour still survives; William Cecil also should be described as one of the queen's favourites, and probably her first, although his services to her were of a purely ministerial nature.

Much of the aura surrounding these favourites emanated from Elizabeth's court, which the queen presided over with a great determination and even strictness, taking much interest even in the conduct of her maids and other domestics. It was a brilliant assemblage of people, moving from palace to palace with the queen herself: Richmond, Westminster, Nonsuch and others. Music was a particular feature, and dancing, which the queen loved to indulge throughout her life, a prominent distraction. As Elizabeth and her courtiers moved from place to place a retinue of musicians and entertainers accompanied them. At court musicians, poets and finally playwrights received gracious and enthusiastic patronage; highly educated and widely read, Elizabeth enjoyed the conversation of thinkers and creative artists, and she expected her courtiers and their wives to match her own inclinations. That to a large extent this civilised trait was realised, resulting among other things in a marked increase in the refinement of the diplomatic sector in London, stands as a lasting tribute to the last of the Renaissance monarchs in England and the last of the Tudors. Elizabeth's court was probably the most brilliant England has ever seen; although many exceptions might be given, it was almost without parallel for the circumstance that virtually every person of consequence who lived during Elizabeth's reign and who resided most frequently in the south of England (Elizabeth herself never journeyed north) had access to the court and in some measure enjoyed royal patronage.

Of Richard Devereux, second Earl of Essex and son of Walter Devereux, much has been written over the years. But as with so many of those who congregated about Elizabeth there came a time when even he was told to 'go and be hanged', being forthwith banished from court. This occurred in 1598; three years later on February 25, 1601, the once dashing earl was executed in the Tower, guilty of high treason. It was an ignominious conclusion to what had promised to be a highly successful career, launched by his guardian Cecil when the latter introduced the young man just down from Trinity College, Cambridge, to Elizabeth's glittering court. There his fine person and good looks soon won him the favour of the queen; and in 1585 his chance came to show his mettle in a military capacity when as General of the Horse he accompanied Leicester to Holland and distinguished himself at the Battle of Zutphen. Promotion followed in 1591 when he commanded the force despatched to assist Henry IV of France in the continued war against Spain.

In 1596 he was selected to accompany Lord Howard in the expedition against Cadiz, then in the following year he was rewarded with the position of Earl Marshal, a seemingly all-powerful and influential position that led the earl to presume too much on his own importance, which in its turn led to his downfall. Temporary restoration to at least a vestige of his former favour came in 1599

EARL OF ESSEX.

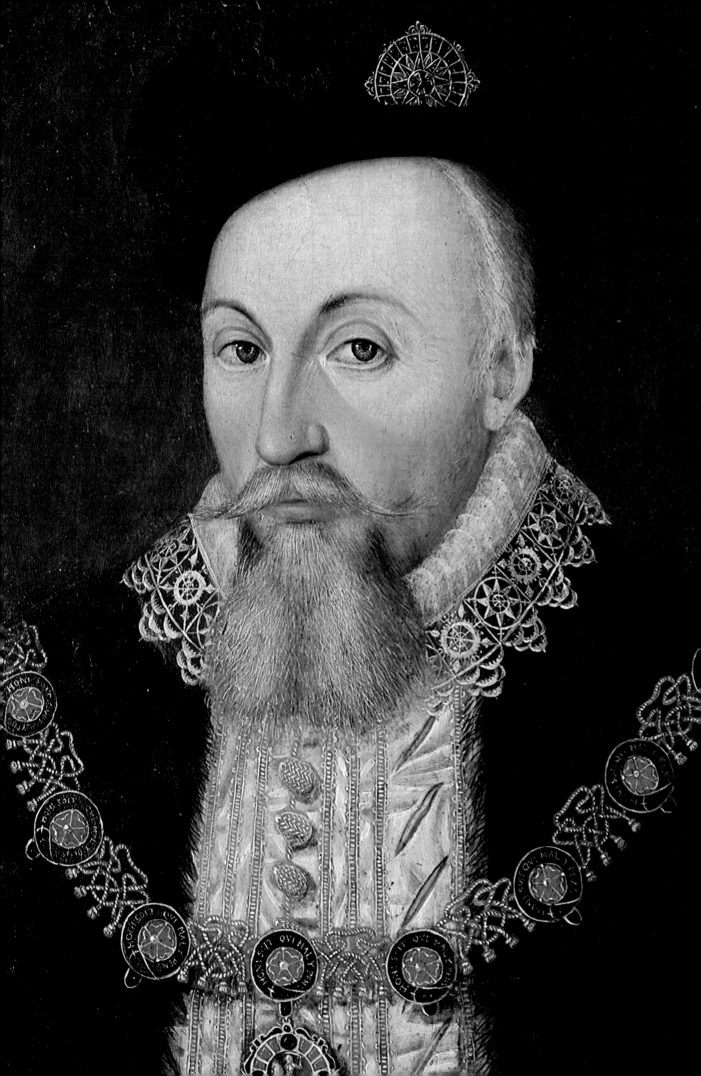

when he was sent to Ireland as Lord Lieutenant, together with an army of 20,000 men with which he hoped to stem the Irish troubles. But here he once more brought disfavour on his own head when he returned to England without permission, his army largely destroyed, as a result of which he was stripped of his remaining dignities. He immediately attempted an insurrection against the queen, and as was of course almost inevitable he failed and lost his head. In his time he was one of the great ornaments of the Elizabethan court, and his end was perhaps in keeping with his impetuous character.

Robert Dudley, Earl of Leicester, was a good deal older than Essex, and indeed he is the man thought to have made the most forceful inroads on the queen's heart. Born in 1531, he was the son of the Duke of Northumberland (Warwick). As Lord Robert Dudley he had stood trial alongside his father over the question of Jane Grey's accession, but had been spared execution and following a year's imprisonment in the Tower had travelled abroad, taking part in the Battle of St. Quentin in which English and Spanish troops were victorious over the French. With the accession of Elizabeth he came back into royal favour: he was made a Knight of the Garter, a Privy Councillor and appointed to the post of Master of the Horse. In 1563 he was created Earl of Leicester.

Many commentators have been of the opinion that Leicester's sole qualification towards advancement was his fine person and that his other accomplishments were few. Until his death in 1588 he was constantly in the queen's company, and as the lovely painting reproduced in these pages of the queen and her subject dancing together amply demonstrates, the two were well matched. Leicester himself was three times wed, the last time to the widow of Walter Devereux, first Earl of Essex and father of Robert Devereux. His death, which occurred during September, was thought to have been as a result of poison, and his last wife is said to have administered it in revenge after he had first prepared it for her consumption.

Leicester was very nearly a complete failure in all matters other than courtly. In 1585, armed with extreme powers, he journeyed to the Low Countries, as mentioned above, and behaved with both insolence and lack of judgment, achieving nothing lasting at all. Despite this, his queen made him commander-in-chief of an army raised in 1588 to meet the expected Spanish invasion of England. 'Sweet Robin', as he was known to his monarch, he has passed into history as one of the most glamorous personalities of his time, his failures being overlooked in the interests of his far more intriguing relationship with the virgin queen.

Perhaps Leicester's Dutch expedition was his least fortunate. England's interference in the Netherlands during 1585 was a direct result of Spanish aggression. When Leicester sailed there in December he went at the head of an army consisting of 6,000 foot soldiers and 1,000 horse. His charge was quite simply to discourage the Spaniards, but on his arrival the Dutch people hailed him and the English queen as saviours, and contrary to Elizabeth's instructions he allowed them to confer upon him the title of Governor and Captain General, almost inferring English sovereignty of the Low Countries, a responsibility Elizabeth did not wish to incur. Leicester showed further traits of imprudence in his mishandling of the large sum of money provided to support his English expeditionary force. In addition he neglected his troops, many of whom went hungry. There were certain victories in this campaign — as at Zutphen — but by and large Leicester showed himself a poor military commander. As in the instance of Essex, it is difficult to perceive how it was that Elizabeth could promote the activities of a man unsuited to high military responsibilities.

opposite:
Robert Dudley, Earl of Leicester. The queen's favourite is here shown wearing the insignia of the Order of the Garter. At his death in 1588 the earldom became extinct, Leicester's property passing to his sister Mary, then married to Sir Henry Sidney of Penshurst, Kent.

Elizabeth's progresses

... the next day she departed thence on her Progress into Essex; and the chief streets of the City being renewed with fresh sand and gravel for her equipage, she passed from Charterhouse through Smithfield, under Newgate; and so along St. Nicholas Shambles, Cheapside, Cornhill, unto Aldgate and White-chapel. All the houses were hung with cloth and arras and rich carpets, and silk; but Cheapside was hung with cloth of gold and silver, and velvets of all colours; all the crafts of London standing in their liveries, from St. Michael the Quern as far as to Aldgate. The cavalcade was after this manner: first, serving men riding; then the Queen's Pensioners, Gentlemen, Knights, Lords, the Aldermen in scarlet, the Serjeants of Arms, the Heralds in their coat armour; then my Lord Mayor bearing the scepter; then the Lord Hunsdon bearing the sword; and then came the Queen's Grace, and her footmen richly habited; the Ladies and Gentlewomen followed; after all, the Lords and Knight's men in their masters liveries; and at the Whitechapel the Lord Mayor and Aldermen took their leave of her Grace; and so she took her way toward Essex, and I suppose lodged that night at Wanstead House in the Forest.

(John Nichols: *The Progresses of Elizabeth*).

The visits paid by Elizabeth to a succession of favoured magnates, with whom she stayed and by whom she was lavishly entertained, reflect an altogether novel aspect of her reign. Elizabeth considered it very important not only to impress her dignity and accomplishments upon the peers of her realm, but also to make contact with its ordinary citizens by travelling in glory among them. Her progresses occupied several weeks at a time (though she never ventured outside the south of England) and incurred considerable expenditure.

The itinerary of an early progress of 1561 into the counties of Essex, Suffolk and Hertfordshire gives a clear impression of what was involved. The queen left London (from Somerset House in the Strand) on July 11 and journeyed to Wanstead where she passed the night at the house of Lord Rich, Lord Chancellor during the reign of Edward VI. The following day she proceeded to the Earl of Oxford's seat at Havering and then the next day to Sir John Grey's seat of Purgo, presented to him by the queen in 1559. Returning to Havering, Elizabeth went next to Lowten Hall, granted to Sir Thomas Darcy by Edward VI, and then passed two nights at Ingatestone, the home of her principal secretary, Sir William Petre, a Privy Councillor who had enjoyed royal favour ever since the days of Henry VIII. Beginning on July 21, five nights were next passed at the royal mansion of New Hall near Boreham, Chelmsford, which Henry VIII had bought from a Bishop of London in 1517, vastly improving the property and naming it Beaulieu.

From Filliot's Hall near Colchester, the home of one Henry Long, the queen entered Colchester itself, where the town corporation presumably undertook its monarch's entertainment. She remained there altogether four nights, breaking her stay by two nights passed at St. Osyth with Lord John Darcy; then she proceeded to Harwich, where she remained four nights, and then to Ipswich for five nights, being probably entertained in both of these towns at the expense of their corporations.

Lord Rich's Shelley Hall near Ongar provided one night's accommodation, the Waldegrave house at Smalbridge a further two. Then Elizabeth spent five nights with Sir Lionel Tollemache at Helmingham near Ipswich, proceeding to two other of Rich's properties, Gosfield and Leez, for six nights further. On Monday, August 15 she progressed to Great Hallingbury, residence of the

opposite:
This painting attributed to Robert Peake and dated c.1600 shows Elizabeth making a public progress towards the close of her reign. Still she endeavoured to present the image of the queen in majesty, lastingly youthful and adored by all her courtiers and followers. Knights of the Order of the Garter immediately precede the queen in this painting, the first seven of them, reading from left to right, being Edmund Sheffield, first Earl of Mulgrave; Charles Howard, Lord Howard of Effingham; George Clifford, third Earl of Cumberland; Thomas Butler, tenth Earl of Ormonde; an unknown courtier; George Talbot, seventh Earl of Shrewsbury; Edward Somerset, fourth Earl of Worcester. The painting has not survived in complete form, having been cut down both at the top and at the sides. Its painter, Robert Peake, who flourished during the last quarter of the sixteenth century and the first quarter of the seventeenth, was one of the most widely sought after artists of his day and produced numerous portraits. Following Elizabeth's death he achieved great prominence at the court of James I. It is of interest to note that the street paving shown here is of wood.

Morley family but then in the possession of George Boleyn, Viscount Rochfort and a relative of the queen. She remained there two nights and then went to Standen in Hertfordshire, seat of Sir Ralph Sadler, Privy Councillor and Chancellor of the Duchy of Lancaster.

Sadler acted as host to his queen for a total of two and a half weeks. Then on September 6 the queen passed to her own palace at Endville, ending her progress on September 12 at St. James' Palace, which had been built at the command of Henry VIII. As will be deduced from this account, in an age when travel by road was by no means comfortable the queen's progresses were arduous undertakings.

As can be inferred from the passage at the head of this section describing the outset of this 1561 progress, Elizabeth's retinue was considerable, its effect deliberately theatrical. Even more so were the entertainments with which the monarch was greeted at certain residences. Masques were the staple fare on these occasions, while numerous orations and praiseful songs greeted the queen as she passed from place to place. One day during 1578 Thomas Churchyard, a minor poet of the time and in charge of all royal entertainments during a progress into Suffolk and Norfolk, was asked by the Lord Chamberlain to provide a surprise entertainment by the roadside to greet the queen as she travelled. Churchyard later published a record of the entertainments he devised during the course of this progress, and although the piece in question was actually prevented from taking place because of rain it is of great interest.

Churchyard caused a hole to be dug in the ground close to a river to represent a water nymphs' pool. This he covered with canvas painted the colour of grass and so arranged that with the aid of cords it could be easily drawn open and

Queen Elizabeth hunting. Taken from Turberville's Book of Hunting *of 1575.*

134

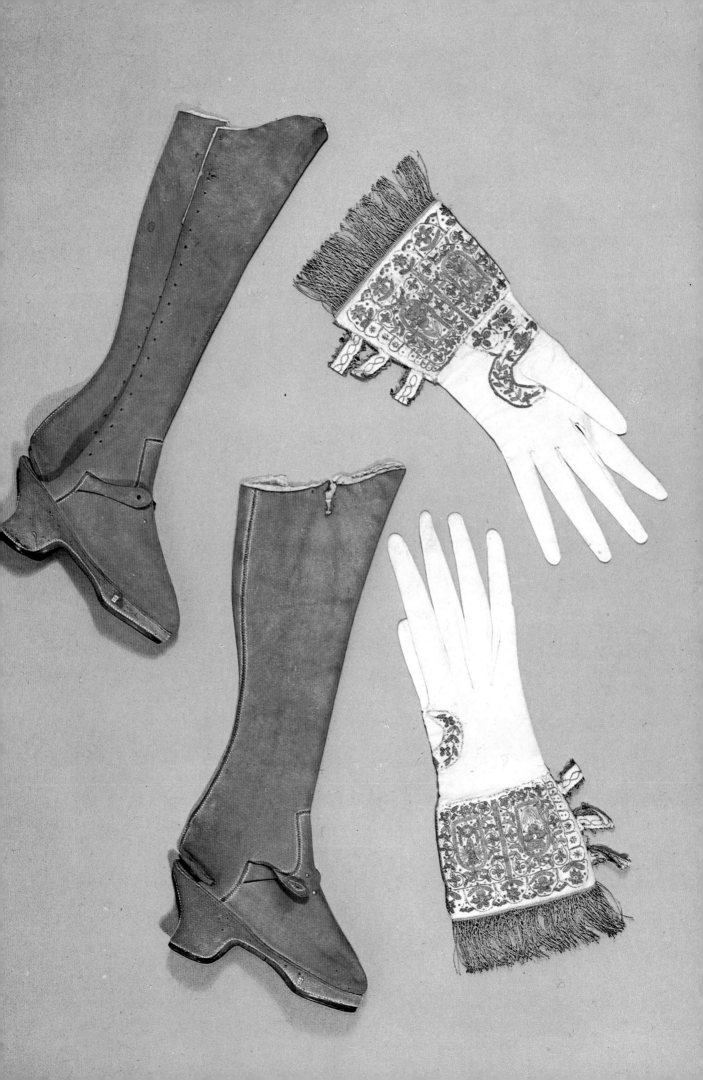

previous page:
Elizabeth I loved to dance, and she particularly liked to dance with her favourite Leicester. This painting by an unknown artist shows the two dancing while courtiers look on. Two viols and a viola da gamba are played by the musicians, while the dance itself is a particularly sprightly one, Leicester having lifted the queen off the ground. The small girl in the foreground acts as a reminder of the position of the child in earlier times, being looked upon as no more than a miniature adult, and painted thus by the artist.

then closed again. Musicians were to be placed inside this 'cave', as well as twelve nymphs 'desguised or dressed most strangely'. The nymphs would in fact have been boys, as was customary at that time. As the queen approached it was intended that a nymph should spring up out of the ground, make obeisance and utter a speech. She was to be followed by three others, and when all four had completed their speeches they were to return to their cave and the music would begin to play. That ended, all twelve nymphs would then come forth and render 'a daunce with timbrels that were trimmed with belles, and other jangling things'. At this point male figures were intended to become visible at a distance, suitors to the boy impersonating Beauty and over whom they were destined to fight with one another, the combat being decided eventually by Fortune.

Elizabeth continued to make progresses until almost the conclusion of her reign, and in all visited almost 150 different worthies on these occasions. Day-to-day household expenses, as well as presents received and given by the sovereign, entailed great extravagance on all sides. Thus, for example, when Elizabeth stayed with Lord North of Kertlinge in 1578, for a period extending from Sunday evening to the following Wednesday, her host was obliged to lay out a sum of £762 4s. 2d. in order to feed and entertain his guests and household, the sum also including what was spent on gifts and gratuities. The items included 74 hogsheads of beer at a cost of £32 7s. 6d., six hogsheads of claret at £27, twenty gallons of sack at £2 13s. 4d., 32 swans at £10 13s. 4d., 34 pigs at only a shilling each, 32 geese at the same cost, four stags and sixteen bucks which were made into a total of 176 'pasties' and a host of other edibles, ranging from gulls, snipe, plovers and curlews to oysters, crayfish (eight dozen) and herring.

From these figures it is possible to suspect that the progresses of Elizabeth both inconvenienced and caused expense to her various hosts. They were however an essential ingredient of her reign and as much as anything else she undertook served to cement the affection of her common subjects for her as they observed her passing in their midst.

Discovery, conquest and colonisation under Elizabeth

O Frobusher! thy bruit and name shal be enrold in bookes,
That whosoever after comes and on they labour lookes,
Shall muse ard marvell at thyne actes, and greatness of thy minde.
I say no more, least some affirme I fanne thy face with winde,
I flatter for affections sake: well, God shall witnesse be,
In this thy prayse (and other bookes) I speake but right of thee.

(A Welcome Home to Master Martin Frobusher, by Thomas Churchyard).

Elizabeth's was the great age of discovery. Drake, Raleigh, Gilbert, Frobisher, Hawkins; their names still have the power to conjure up admiration. Elizabeth personally encouraged their activities, saw the value of trade conducted on an international level — which led towards the close of her reign to the founding of the East India Company — and of the process of colonisation. Yet it is strange that with the exception of the exploits of the Cabots towards the close of Henry VII's reign very little had been accomplished before this time by the English; while the Spanish as a result were already enjoying a brisk commerce from their south and central American activities.

Closely allied with the growth in trade and discovery that blossomed in Elizabeth's time was the consolidation of English sea power; and whereas discovery and colonisation can be traced directly to an increase in trading generally, the rise in naval supremacy can be easily attributed to a desire to antagonise Spanish mariners, whose monarch was England's adversary. Buccaneering, indeed, became almost an accredited industry.

England's own exports continued to comprise mainly wool and cloth (they amounted to almost 80% of all exports). The newly formed Muscovy Company opened up new trading possibilities with the east, but initially only with the Russians, though exploratory voyages began to be made with a view to opening up other markets. Anthony Jenkinson made two overland voyages to the Asian continent, in 1557 and 1561, in quest of new trading contacts.

The great impetus to overseas exploration came with the publication of Humphrey Gilbert's *Discourse to Prove a North-West Passage,* in which the old (and discarded) notion of a passage through the Arctic to the east was revived. Gilbert proved to his own satisfaction, with reference to every available published source (none of them possessing any credence), that such a passage not only could but did exist. Martin Frobisher and many others were swayed by Gilbert's argument. The first voyage to be undertaken in this new

opposite:
The entertainment given before Elizabeth at Elvetham, Hampshire, home of the Earl of Hertford, in 1591. One of the most lavish entertainments devised for the monarch, this particular one took the form of an aquatic display in an ornamental pond close to the earl's house, a canopied throne of green velvet being set up for the queen beside the lake. Once seated Elizabeth was approached by a succession of marine deities who swam or walked through the water pulling a craft bearing three virgins and a sea nymph. Also in the craft were two jewels to be presented to her majesty. Songs, orations and various feats followed throughout the day. As the illustration shows, the pond was also adorned with many artificial features, including a castle; while on the right, lettered 'G', was a 'Snayl Mount' that changed in time into a 'monster, having hornes full of wild-fire, continually burning'. As with many such entertainments on these occasions, the description and songs were published as a 'tract', being twice printed during 1591. This illustration, newly engraved in 1822 for another purpose, appeared in the original tract and was hand coloured.

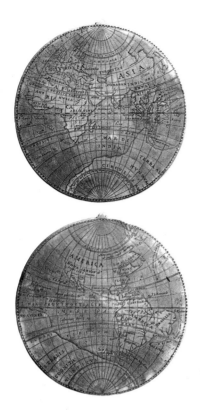

Drake's circumnavigation of the world in 1577-80 was commemorated in 1586 by the striking of a silver medal based upon Michael Mercator's map of the world. The eastern hemisphere is shown on one side, the western on the other, Drake's course being delineated by a dotted line. Drake's findings were incorporated in Mercator's map, while the part of the world explored by Frobisher in 1576-78 is also correctly shown.

The Elizabethan mariner Sir John Hawkins, whose activities along the African coast in securing cargoes of negroes, for use as slaves in Spanish south America, did much to foster the slave trade. His first such voyage was made during the autumn of 1562 and a second two years later. His profits on both occasions were high. Spanish opposition to the ease with which he accomplished his designs however grew, and the violence he encountered on his third voyage in 1567 heralded the Spanish-English rivalry that would only culminate in the defeat of the Spanish Armada in 1588.

right:
Sir Humphrey Gilbert, author of the influential Discourse to Prove a North-West Passage. In 1578 it was Gilbert who secured a patent from Elizabeth to colonise America.

wave of exploration was led by Frobisher during the period 1576-78, with the personal backing of the queen, Burghley, Leicester and others and under the patronage of the Earl of Warwick. The whole enterprise was kept secret from the Spaniards, and even though Frobisher returned with no success story to recount traders did not abandon their encouragement of the quest.

In 1580 another expedition was despatched, with the purpose this time of discovering the north-east passage, but never again during Elizabeth's reign was this particular challenge taken up. The failure of this latter mission did not however dampen the enthusiasm of traders in the east, and as a result of a visit by William Harborne to Sultan Murad III of Turkey English merchants were granted sole trading rights in Turkey, leading in 1581 to the founding of the Levant Company, awarded a charter by the queen. Then India and Burma too became trading objectives with English merchants, leading to a nine year expedition by land and sea accomplished by Ralph Fitch, who left England in 1583 in the company of John Newbery (who perished in the endeavour). The perils of a journey such as this in many ways exceeded those of a sea voyage and Fitch's accomplishment was very considerable.

Meanwhile John Davis continued the search for a north-west passage. Between 1585 and 1587 he made three separate voyages. On the third of these he gained a latitude of 73 degrees, an apparently open sea lying before him; but unfortunately it was ice-ridden. He concluded that he was looking out at the north-west passage and that in better conditions it could be breached. This was the last attempt made in Elizabeth's time to discover the mythical passage; instead English minds were diverted to the question of establishing a colony in north America (Gilbert had set sail in 1583 with a view to reconnoitring the land, perishing at sea while sailing southwards beside the as yet unknown coast of what is today the United States).

Sir John Hankins Kt.

M. rd. Gucht Sculp

Quid Non

Sir Humphrey Gilbert, Kt.

THE
HISTORIE OF
THE WORLD
IN FIVE BOOKES.

Ntreating of the Beginning and first Ages of the same, from the Creation unto Abraham.

2 Of the Times from the Birth of Abraham to the destruction of the Temple of Salomon.

3 From the destruction of Jerusalem, to the time of Philip of Macedon.

4 From the Raigne of Philip of Macedon, to the establishing of that Kingdome in the Race of Antigonus.

5 From the settled rule of Alexanders Successors in the East, untill the Romans (prevailing over all) made Conquest of Asia and Macedon.

By Sir WALTER RALEIGH, Knight.

One of the most outstanding explorers of Elizabethan times also made a marked contribution to the literature of the day, and under particularly distressing circumstances. Sir Walter Raleigh wrote his Historie of the World *while imprisoned in the Tower for a period of thirteen years, having been reprieved from a sentence of death. Although projected to continue down to his own times, Raleigh in fact reached only Roman times; even so, the resultant folio is extremely lengthy. It was published in 1614. Raleigh finally met his death on the executioner's block on October 29, 1618, having the evening before written the famous poem which begins 'Go, soul, the body's guest'.*

opposite:
An astrolabe manufactured in 1588 and sometimes said to have belonged to Sir Francis Drake. To the Elizabethan mariner the astrolabe served as the principal aid to navigation.

Gilbert's death pointed the way for Sir Walter Raleigh, who in 1584 headed a scheme to continue with the project. The following year Sir Richard Grenville was despatched with a band of settlers, over a hundred of whom elected to stay in Florida. They were re-provisioned by Grenville's ships the year following, but for a number of reasons, including the enmity of the Indian natives, they decided to return home when Drake visited them on his way back from the West Indies. In 1587 Raleigh despatched a second hundred settlers to America, this time under the captaincy of John White, making for what is now Virginia.

This band of settlers apparently perished at the hands of the Indian population. Raleigh himself must have been a bitterly disappointed man. His impetuousness — which was finally to cost him his head — made no allowances for the precaution of careful consideration. Elizabethan colonisation, in part because of military matters which were soon to occupy its principals and in part because of the essential spirit of hurriedness of the age, came almost to naught. The vision however, of an empire across the sea, continued to attract men of the time.

Sir Francis Drake, surely the giant among Elizabethan mariners, took up the question of operating on the American continent — in his case mainly south America — in quite a different manner. He had long been at odds with the Spaniards, operating piratically about the Panama isthmus in the early 1570's, seizing Spanish treasure and as a result incurring Elizabeth's favour. Following his success in this sphere he conceived the notion of a circumnavigation of the globe. Undoubtedly a part of his motive was to discover new means of harassing Spanish ships, but he also had at heart the ideal of establishing colonies in what is now California. Drake's circumnavigation in the *Golden Hind* was accomplished between 1577 and 1580, and in addition to this nautical feat he returned to England the successful ravager of many Spanish craft, unloading plunder at the end of his voyage said to have been to the value of £1,500,000, a considerable portion of the entire annual yield of Philip II's mines in southern America. Drake's principal ancillary achievement in his circumnavigation was to sail as far south as latitude 57 in the Pacific, having entered the ocean by way of the Magellan Strait (although his penetrating thus far south was accidental and due entirely to storm conditions). From there he pursued a northerly course up the western coast of the two American continents as far as what is today San Francisco before sailing west and passing around the entire globe. Cavendish, who followed Drake during the period 1586-88, pursued a similar course, likewise returning with a large cargo of captured Spanish treasure.

Drake's voyage marked the high point of discovery and navigation during Elizabeth's reign. With the temporary abandonment of the ambition to found an English colony in north America more stress was placed on continuing the expansion of trade with the east, culminating in 1599 with the founding of the East India Company, whose status over two centuries later had become almost sovereign. Apart from this, however, nautical activity during the latter part of Elizabeth's reign was destined to be of a military character.

The Elizabethan stage

Complaints having been made to the Council generally of the disorders occasioned by stage plays, and especially against the building of the new house in Golding Lane by Edward Alleyn, sundry restrictions are now laid upon them . . . Nevertheless, because of the many particular abuses and disorders that do ensue, it is now ordered that two houses, and no more, shall be allowed, the Globe upon the Bankside for the use of the Lord Chamberlain's servants, and this new house for my Lord Admiral's men, but lest it add to the number of playhouses the Curtain shall be plucked down or put to some other use. Moreover, these two companies shall play twice a week only and no oftener, and especially they shall refrain to play on the Sabbath day, and shall forbear

altogether in time of Lent. Further the Lord Mayor and the justices of the peace of Middlesex and Surrey are charged with the execution of these orders.

(Act of the Privy Council, June 22, 1600).

The Elizabethan stage was greatly different from that of the twentieth century, the habit of playgoing certainly a much less sedate pastime. Even so, 'modern' drama dates from this era, from the time of Shakespeare, Marlowe, Ben Jonson, Beaumont and Fletcher and many others. In one year — 1576 — three theatres were built in London, among them the famous Globe. From that time forward it is true to say that Elizabethan drama constituted one of the principal creative activities of the time.

Until 1576 no public theatres at all had existed in London; the drama itself had consisted entirely either of exercises in pageantry or else seasonal ecclesiastical dramas. All at once, and in a comparatively short period of growth, the national drama was established. The origins can perhaps be assigned to the year 1574, when the Earl of Leicester became patron of the first permanent company of players ever to be assembled. Professional playwrights — who might otherwise have been propounders of unpopular beliefs in more conventional form but saw in the drama a means whereby they could air their grievances under the cloak of humour — were quick to take advantage of the new entertainment. Thomas Kyd and Christopher Marlowe were among the earliest of the new wave of writers, although they followed in the wake of such now little heard of innovators as John Lyly.

Marlowe's name has survived through the centuries as much because of its owner's personal history — knifed to death in a tavern brawl — as because of his great talent. He was the author of such frequently represented plays as *Tamburlaine the Great, The History of Doctor Faustus* and *The Jew of Malta.* The tragedy of Marlowe's career is that had he not met the violent death he did he would undoubtedly have faced persecution, and possibly execution, on account of his atheistical leanings. In his plays he was able to present certain of

Mr. WILLIAM
SHAKESPEARES
COMEDIES,
HISTORIES, &
TRAGEDIES.

Publiſhed according to the True Originall Copies.

L O N D O N
Printed by Iſaac Iaggard, and Ed. Blount. 1623.

his views as though merely the opinions of his stage characters; in his personal statements he was less discreet and incurred the displeasure of many. Marlowe proclaimed openly that in his opinion there was no God, and even in an age when the comparative oppressiveness of Mary's reign had given way to realistic tolerance he could not expect to escape recrimination for airing such thoughts as this. A product of the universities, an intellectual and a man of mettle, Marlowe died in 1593 at the age of 29. His plays were those of a man of considerable culture, and they lent great respectability to the profession of dramatist.

Marlowe's standing as a man of education and never a common 'player' (a species accorded but scant social recognition) was a stark contrast to his great contemporary and successor. It is of no mean interest to note that this successor himself has occasionally been written off as no more than a player whose name was employed as a mask for a Marlowe who had recovered from his tavern wounds but did not wish the fact to be made known. This successor was of course William Shakespeare of Stratford-upon-Avon, who after he had achieved recognition was received by the queen and enjoyed her patronage. That Francis Bacon and others have also been advanced as the true authors of Shakespeare's plays surely serves to indicate that Marlowe did die when he is supposed to have done and that Shakespeare almost certainly was the author of his own plays.

Shakespeare was born on April 23, 1564. He was not yet twenty years of age when he left his native Stratford to gain a livelihood in London, first of all as an attendant at the Globe Theatre in Southwark. He progressed to the rank of actor, later becoming a writer and appearing in several of his own early plays (he played the Ghost in his own drama of *Hamlet*). Success attended the playwright, so that in 1589 he was able to become co-proprietor of the Blackfriars Theatre. A poet as well as playwright, Shakespeare has long been regarded as the supreme writer in the history of English literature; the royal patronage he enjoyed during Elizabeth's reign survived into Stuart times and the court of James I. The playwright died in 1616, the details of his life virtually unrecorded.

If any one dramatist can typify the position of the artist in Renaissance England it is undoubtedly Shakespeare: his acceptance at the court of Elizabeth was based entirely on his talents. The related acceptance of the regular stage in London was a further indication of the considerable degree of freedom of expression then prevalent. But of equal importance as a dramatist was Ben Jonson, and the title of one of his principal dramas — *Bartholomew Fair* — is a reminder of a quite different form of public entertainment popular during Elizabethan times.

Numerous fairs were held in different parts of London that were at that time still outlying villages like Mayfair, as well as south of the river in Southwark. They were annual events, extending sometimes for as long as two weeks. At these fairs, as well as marketing, pickpocketing and dancing, were to be found 'booths' in which garbled forms of drama were purveyed. Sometimes unsavoury, the fairs enjoyed the patronage of aristocracy and peasantry alike.

Jonson, who wrote in such lively fashion of Bartholomew Fair, was ten years Shakespeare's junior, and died in 1637. He was educated at Westminster School under William Camden, who wrote the history of Elizabeth's reign. A protegé of Shakespeare, his first successful comedy, *Every Man in his Humour,* was produced in 1598. In the firmament of Elizabethan dramatists Jonson cannot therefore be said to occupy a prominent place, for his principal period of production was during the reign of James I. He was, though, very much a product of his times and almost the last of the great dramatists to practise in this country before the suppression of the theatres by Cromwell. With the restoration in 1660 a new form of drama altogether was introduced to London.

Elizabethan playhouses were built after a plan entirely their own, being circular in construction and with the pit area open to the elements. In this pit, occasionally on benches but more often standing, playgoers lounged while a performance was in progress. Talking, eating and drinking, movement from one vantage point to another and active encouragement or criticism of actors were all the order of the day. In galleries around the pit other spectators enjoyed slightly less rowdy conditions (normally there would be three tiers of galleries). The stage was what is known as an 'apron stage', jutting out into the pit. Here, without aid of lighting (performances always took place in daylight), actors performed dramas in the ordinary dress of their day. At the rear of the stage was a curtained-off area suitable for interior scenes and above this an upper storey or balcony allowing considerable realism when performers were required to be variously deployed. Above this again was the 'heaven', where mechanical suns, moons and clouds could be brought into play; while the stage itself was hollow, allowing easy trapdoor work. Nobody has yet satisfactorily reconstructed an Elizabethan stage, for no complete specifications have survived. Among the various attempts to physically reproduce such a stage perhaps the theatre at the Folger Shakespeare Library in Washington is the most pleasing.

Many other arts flourished during the Elizabethan era, and almost all of them could look to the queen for encouragement. However, although painting and music, for example, could claim fairly strong links with the immediate past, drama flourished in Elizabeth's time, in its new form, virtually unheralded. To this extent the works of Shakespeare and his small number of contemporary luminaries in this sphere were as expressive of the daring spirit of the age as the exploits of Drake, the glamour of the queen herself or the great growth in naval power.

The continuing fortunes of Cecil

This judgment I have of you, that you will not be corrupted with any manner of gifts, and that you will be faithful to the state.

(Elizabeth I to Cecil upon appointing him Chief Secretary of State, November 20, 1558).

The way in which William Cecil retained the favour of his queen demonstrated yet another aspect of the new climate that was instituted by Elizabeth. Earlier ministers to Elizabeth's predecessors who had won their sovereign's grace had fallen with considerable frequency: Cecil did not, and only on a very few occasions did he incur his queen's disfavour. In the process of consolidating his power and influence he also became immensely wealthy, although he spent most of what came his way. A good deal of this money was devoted to erecting one of the most magnificent country residences built during the Elizabethan period, to be rivalled only by such comparatively smaller structures as Montacute House in Somerset. This he named Burghley House, lying just to the south of Stamford and built on the site of his earlier residence. Among the Secretary of State's motives in building such a magnificent house was to provide a place to entertain his sovereign as often as she wished to travel that far north. He expected her to visit him frequently, and was greatly disappointed that she came to Burghley House only three times.

The Cecils were to pass forward through history in a variety of notable guises. Numerous ministers and other dignitaries bore the name over the ensuing centuries, and even during the nineteenth century a Cecil — Lord Melbourne — was to become Prime Minister, the approximate position which his ancestor William Cecil had occupied.

Burghley House, William Cecil's grandiose residence.

Burghley, who became Lord Treasurer in 1572, was at the helm of English affairs from the very beginning of Elizabeth's reign, and with the exception of a short period during which Robert Dudley appeared to be in danger of replacing him he suffered no loss of power. His contribution to history during his later years is aptly summed up in the words of the author of his entry in the

Dictionary of National Biography: 'To follow his career from this point to its close would be to write the history of England; for by him, more than by any other single man during the last thirty years of his life, was the history of England shaped'. Elizabeth was truly grateful to Cecil for his services, and it is said that never until the day of her own death could she hear mention of the name of the man she had so often call her 'spirit' or 'leviathan' but she shed a tear.

Cecil's accomplishments were legion. Many commentators have been inclined to term the reign of Elizabeth the reign of Cecil, and indeed the historian Froude summed the matter up well by proclaiming 'she was a woman and a man: she was herself and Cecil'. This being the case, it was not unnatural that he should play a significant role in the reform of the Church during his lifetime. Thus although an Archbishop of Canterbury might be appointed, the true controller of Church affairs was Cecil, with the queen herself offering periodic interference. Matthew Parker, who held the see of Canterbury from 1559 to 1579 is reported as complaining towards the end of his life: 'what is it to govern cumbered with such subtilty'.

In foreign affairs also Cecil played an active and significant role, being fully acquainted with the affairs of Europe. In an age when continental sovereigns and their ministers signed and counter-signed alliances indiscriminately and unmeaningly, it was clearly an achievement to be able to steer a wise and justifiable course for as long as he did. Throughout the troubles with France that characterised the early years of Elizabeth's reign, the disagreements with Philip II of Spain that resulted in the Armada, the vexing problems of the Netherlands, ostensibly under Philip's control, and finally the bothersome and rebellious instincts of the Scots and Irish that seemed to dog every English monarch, Cecil was there to counsel, intrigue and seek out solutions. He worked

The canopy of Elizabeth I's bed at Burghley House, believed not to have been occupied since the monarch's last visit to this residence. The decorations and hangings seen here are the original ones and amply demonstrate the lavishness expended upon this house by its builder.

151

opposite:
Mary, Queen of Scots, a panel
painted after the manner of
Hilliard.

with extreme diligence, the great number of his surviving papers still eloquently testifying to his profound capacity for sustained hard work, and by any account he is one of England's greatest statesmen.

Mary, Queen of Scots

And whereas also, sithen the same sentence and judgment so given and recorded, the lords and commons in this present parliament assembled have also at sundry times in open parliament heard and considered the principal evidences, proofs, and circumstances whereupon the same sentence and judgment was grounded, and have, by their public assent in parliament, affirmed the same to be a just, lawful, and true sentence, and so have allowed and approved the same in writing presented unto us, and have also notified to us how deeply they did foresee the great and many imminent dangers which otherwise might and would grow to our person and to the whole realm if this sentence were not fully executed; and consequently therefore they did (by their most humble and earnest petitions in that behalf, of one accord, having access unto us upon their sundry requests, most instantly upon their knees) pray, beseech, and, with many reasons of great force and importance, move and press us that the said sentence and judgment, so justly and duly given and by them approved as is aforesaid, might (according to the express tenor of the said act of parliament) by our proclamation under our Great Seal be declared and published, and the same also finally executed.

(Proclamation upon the sentence against Mary, Queen of Scots, by Elizabeth I, Richmond, December 4, 1586).

One of Elizabeth's most consistent troubles came from Scotland, whose leaders had plagued her Tudor predecessors unceasingly. Her cousin Mary, born in 1542, granddaughter of James IV of Scotland and Henry VIII's sister, Margaret Tudor, presented a particularly unhappy problem for the English queen. This problem culminated in Mary's execution, as well as some particularly unsavoury crimes. Technically Mary was a Stuart; her Tudor ancestry however needs no elucidation.

Mary had been married to Francis II of France as a means of consolidating the Franco-Scottish alliance. On Francis' death she made the fatal decision to return to Scotland, a land that, compared with the sophistication she had known at the court of France, must have seemed primitive and unprepossessing. The only advantage she could hope to gain by returning to her native land was the acquisition of the Scottish crown; she had in addition some claim to the throne of England, and it was arguably no less direct than that of her cousin Elizabeth who had still not negated the 'illegitimate' nature of her birth. Certainly Mary could with justification look upon herself as heir presumptive to the English crown.

Mary was not the staid and well educated person her cousin was. Her ways were those of the French court and her interests tended to verge on the side of

flippancy; indeed, it was in part because of her Frenchness that her return was not looked forward to by the natives of Scotland, who when she landed there in August, 1561 greeted her without enthusiasm. It did not however take her long to gain the good opinion of her subjects; and her only fault perhaps, in the long run, was to take insufficient notice of their points of view.

Having arrived in Scotland Mary at once began to consider her position with regard to the English throne. The Treaty of Edinburgh between England and France, signed on July 6, 1560, had bound both powers to forsake interference in the affairs of the northern kingdom, Mary of Guise (widow of James V) and a force of French soldiers withdrawing from Scotland at the same time. In recognising Mary Stuart as Queen of Scotland the treaty had also required her to disown all claim to the English throne. Mary's first goal therefore was to secure amendment to this particular clause.

Initial approaches to Elizabeth seemed favourable enough. On the other hand, taking into account her experience before she had come to the throne, the English monarch was easily capable of perceiving that public knowledge of Mary's right of inheritance could, if the Scot was to become popular, lead to a violent decline in her own fortunes. In this eminently sensible assessment of the situation lay the seeds of Mary's downfall. To ensure stability in her own lifetime Elizabeth affirmed that while she yet lived she would assign no heir to her crown, and that when she died the person with the greatest claim to it must make his or her own individual move.

Mary then suggested a meeting with the English queen, and this was duly arranged to take place at Nottingham; it was however postponed at Elizabeth's instigation at the last moment. To Mary this was something of a setback, especially as her uncle the Duke of Guise had been partly instrumental in influencing Elizabeth's decision. Mary's next ploy therefore was to project a powerful marriage for herself, in the hope that such an arrangement would consolidate her claim in the English queen's eyes. Having long been appreciative of this contingency, Elizabeth in turn had to ensure that Mary did not marry any of her own continental antagonists or their close relatives; and she would have preferred it if Mary was to seek out a husband among the English aristocracy. That Mary had designs on the heir to the Spanish throne, Don Carlos, was particularly distressing to Elizabeth.

The English queen suggested her own favourite, the Earl of Leicester, and with a view to this Mary asked for a meeting between her own ministers and those of Elizabeth. Then another solution presented itself, for Matthew, Earl of Lennox (son-in-law of Margaret Tudor) returned to Scotland and was followed by his son Henry, Lord Darnley. The English realisation that Mary was interested in Darnley spurred Elizabeth and Cecil to project the Leicester match with even greater force; Cecil went so far as to suggest that Mary's marriage to the English favourite would ensure their joint right to the English throne on Elizabeth's death.

Despite all Cecil's intrigue and Elizabeth's promise, Mary eventually opted to marry Darnley — much to the disquiet of many Scottish noblemen. Elizabeth's reaction was to demand the return of Darnley (now Earl of Ross and Duke of Rothesay) to England; but certain Scottish nobles did in fact support Mary and Darnley, and on July 29, 1564 the two were married, both parties having an equal claim on the English throne through their common grandmother. As a result of the match rebellion rose in Scotland, though Mary's troops quelled it in little over two months.

With relations between the two British kingdoms as they were, war had now become a possibility; nor would Mary necessarily be in the weaker position, her Roman Catholic allies on the continent being ever ready to come to her assistance. Money came from the Pope, and troops, though never forthcoming, were promised from Spain, and it began to seem that Mary would be willing to launch a military attack on England in order to gain its crown. She was now pregnant, and although her future child was destined to assume the crown of England it was to be by peaceful means and not for several decades to come. Her disadvantage lay in the discovery that the man she had married was both weak and a wastrel; moreover there were exiled and rebellious Scots lords who would have agreed to the powerless Darnley assuming Scottish rule if they could then manipulate him to their own advantages. For his part Darnley thoroughly approved this latter course.

The conspiracy against Mary began with the murder of her Italian secretary, David Rizzio; but Darnley, taken for a fool even by his co-conspirators in this deed, did not gain his desired advancement. Finally, in September, 1566, he announced his intention of leaving Scotland for good. The birth of Prince James had somewhat consolidated Mary's position, and had raised again the question

opposite:
The Oxburgh Hangings. Now preserved in the Victoria and Albert Museum in London, these fragments of tapestry were worked by Mary, Queen of Scots, and Bess of Hardwick, who was then married to George Talbot, the Earl of Shrewsbury. Mary was kept in captivity under Salisbury's surveillance at Sheffield Castle from 1569 to 1585. Although her confinement allowed her great leisure and a considerable degree of luxury (she was occasionally allowed to reside elsewhere while her apartments were being cleaned), she suffered a good deal of tedium. These hangings date from about 1570 and depict various creatures, both mythical and real. Reading clockwise from the top left hand corner the outer ones are respectively: 'Poole Snyte', 'Cock of the Alpes', 'Quayle', Peacock, 'Shofler', 'Geno Skyn', Sea Monster, 'Boate Fishe', floral panel, cactus, fragment, 'Water Owle', 'Great Munkey', Elephant. The central panel shows sea monsters and ships.

of the English succession. The disposal of Darnley was thus uppermost in the minds of Mary's advisers. Darnley, who had not followed his promise to leave, returned to Holyrood House, where his son then was, and on February 10, 1567 he was strangled.

Whether or not Mary was directly culpable in the plot against Darnley's life has long been a matter for debate; certainly she knew what was in the air and made no move to prevent the action. This event was destined to be the direct cause of her downfall. Bothwell, one of Mary's favourites and already suspected of being her lover, was the principal suspect and Elizabeth and others wrote to Mary advising her to hasten the enquiry into her husband's death, although none of their letters had any effect. Mary's answer was to create Bothwell Duke of Orkney and marry him on May 15, Bothwell obtaining a divorce to make this possible.

Mary's happiness with her new husband did not endure long. Those who believed in his guilt were determined to bring him to account. Mary's own subjects turned against her and her unpopularity was manifest. Bothwell fled to Denmark, only to be imprisoned there, dying in 1578. Mary surrendered to her persecutors and was imprisoned in Loch Leven Castle. Clearly her life was now in danger, and with it the whole question of the Scottish succession. Elizabeth of England, determined to see justice done, despatched her ambassador Sir Nicholas Throckmorton to Edinburgh in July, 1567 and threatened war if Mary should be executed unjustifiably. As a result of this Mary abdicated from the throne in favour of her son, who became James VI, though Mary remained in captivity.

On May 2, 1568 Mary succeeded in escaping, her supporters entering into hostilities on her behalf. They were however defeated and Mary fled to England, presenting Elizabeth with an extremely delicate situation, Mary obviously hoping that English troops would come to her assistance in helping her to regain the Scottish throne. The English solution was to keep Mary captive until the question of Darnley's murder had been finally solved, and then at her acquittal to allow her into Elizabeth's presence.

Elizabeth forced Mary to agree to three conditions: firstly to abandon any claim to the English throne during Elizabeth's time, secondly to renounce the alliance with France and form one instead with England, and finally to introduce Protestant worship into Scotland in place of Catholicism following her restoration, if it should take place. With Mary's acquiescence in these matters a so-called 'conference' — really a trial — was arranged at York for October, 1568, Mary's Scottish accusers putting their case before an English tribunal headed by the Duke of Norfolk.

Matters reached deadlock at York, and then James Stuart, Earl of Murray (now regent of Scotland but earlier one of Darnley's co-conspirators), revealed the contents of the 'casket letters', a series of letters which had passed between Mary and Bothwell while Darnley was still alive, causing Elizabeth to order the tribunal's removal to Westminster. There, although Mary was not allowed to be present, Murray affirmed that Bothwell had been Darnley's murderer, and that Mary was equally culpable because of her foreknowledge and acquiescence.

No final decision was however reached, the only outcome being the proviso that Mary should remain a prisoner in England. For Elizabeth, Mary's long period of captivity (nineteen years) was to prove a continuing burden and worry: far from appearing in the light of disgrace Mary slowly acquired the status of martyrdom.

Over the long years Mary became involved in numerous intrigues that were embarrassing to her English 'sister'; in a moment of desperation Elizabeth even went so far as to consider Mary's forcible restoration to the Scottish throne. Mary's life had been demanded long enough for her various misdemeanours, but always Elizabeth had spared her, not liking to authorise the execution of a

opposite:
Henry Stuart, Lord Darnley, at the age of seventeen, depicted with his younger brother Charles in 1563.

RANCIS
WALSINGH

princess of the royal blood. Yet still Mary rebuffed Elizabeth by asserting her claim to the English throne. While in captivity the Scottish queen continued to enjoy the revenue of her own dowry, and lived in considerable splendour. Although restricted in her movements she was able to maintain a network of ambassadors, schemers and informers; her correspondence with the Vatican and European rulers continued unabated, her sole resolve being to bring about Elizabeth's downfall, and this Elizabeth cannot have been unaware of. Plots for the queen's murder were unearthed, and invariably Mary could be distantly implicated. Two separate plotters went to their deaths on the scaffold, but Mary was spared, though her captivity was made more secure.

The exile's fall came through her continued endeavours in this direction — via one Anthony Babington who planned to kill Elizabeth — and the cunning of Sir Francis Walsingham, who had been instrumental in depriving Mary of virtually all contact with the outside world (from her latest place of captivity at Chartley in Derbyshire) and then in leading her to believe she had discovered an uninterceptable method of despatching and receiving correspondence.

Babington wrote to Mary early in July, 1586 craving her support in his plot; on July 17 Mary replied giving her approval. Her letter was intercepted and her fate sealed, just as Walsingham had intended (he even forged a postscript to Mary's letter requesting the names of Babington's accomplices).

Babington and his associates were duly arrested, but for a while Mary was not, being confined instead to the royal castle of Fotheringhay in Northampton-shire. Finally Mary was brought to trial, before 36 dignitaries, on October 11, 1586. Refused the aid of counsel, she conducted her own defence as was usual in treason trials. She did this with great credit; but the evidence against her could hardly be contradicted. Yet even at this late stage Elizabeth forbade the court to pass judgment, and it was only after due consideration that parliament approached her on November 12 to demand a 'just sentence'. The queen could not bring herself to confirm a sentence of death, but when she finally did so joyous Londoners celebrated with great enthusiasm. Elizabeth's signature was finally applied to the death warrant on February 1, 1587. She still did not wish to deliver up the instrument of condemnation, however, and finally Burghley did it for her without her knowledge, Mary being informed on February 7 that she was to die the following day.

The Scots queen prepared for death with equanimity; she met it early in the morning with courage. Elizabeth raged (at any rate outwardly) against those who, she said, had acted against her will, particularly Burghley, and to the very last she insisted that she had never wished the Scots princess to die. In part because of Elizabeth's contrition Mary was buried in Peterborough Cathedral in a public ceremony and with full royal honours.

opposite:
Sir Francis Walsingham, painted by an unknown artist. Born in 1536, Walsingham was appointed a Secretary of State and knighted in 1573. He sat as one of the judges at Mary's trial, was honoured with the Order of the Garter in 1587 but died a poor man three years later. A schemer, Walsingham served his queen by acting on her behalf abroad, and it was said that at one time he had 53 spies and 18 additional agents placed in the courts of foreign powers.

Publishing in Elizabethan England

The Queen, having used the services of Mr. William Camden, schoolmaster, in things wherein he has attained skill and intending to employ him again, desireth him to be settled somewhere near her, and eased of the charge of living. She hath required the Dean of Westminster to admit Mr. Camden to the table of the Dean and prebends, and allow him diet for one service; this to be granted for life. The grant she will have sent to her that she may herself present it to Mr. Camden as a token of her gratitude.

(April 4, 1594).

If printing developed in England during the reign of Henry VII and increased in significance during that of Henry VIII, it quite flourished during the reign of Elizabeth I. New editions of the Bible continued to play a significant part in publishing activities (although certain English editions of the Bible were in fact printed abroad, for instance at Antwerp), while philosophical and general religious works had gained a considerable foothold. During the reign of Henry VIII, the 'Renaissance Prince', editions of classical authors too had been published. But during the reign of Elizabeth, in addition to purely literary speculations, the Renaissance spirit manifested itself in the world of publishing by a succession of significant works of history and topography.

That Elizabeth herself acted as both patron and encourager of these enterprises is apparent, and the tally of books is highly impressive: Hakluyt's *Voyages*, Michael Drayton's *Poly Olbion*, Holinshed's *Chronicles*, Camden's *Annales*, Stow's *Survey of London* and Hall's *Chronicle*, to mention but a few of the more significant titles. The urge to record for posterity, abetted by the huge advances in printing techniques, was a typical Renaissance concept, while such publications as Hakluyt's *Voyages* go far towards epitomising the Elizabethan spirit of adventure that did so much for the aggrandisement of the reign of the last of the Tudors.

Richard Hakluyt the younger's *Principal Navigations, Voyages, Traffics and Discoveries of the English Nation* was first published in 1589 and later several times reprinted. It comprised accounts of the numerous important voyages of discovery preceding its publication. A vast compilation in two volumes, it included not only descriptive and historical narratives but also much documentary evidence in the way of official despatches and traders' accounts; in addition it attempted to present all interested in navigational matters with such information as was available to Hakluyt concerning tides, currents and other nautical intelligence. Today the book is of antiquarian interest; Hakluyt himself intended it originally as a book of factual value, and indeed it long served that purpose.

Ralph Holinshed, whose two fat folio volumes were published in 1577 under the title of his *Chronicles*, compiled a history of England from 1066 until his own time, one of the most ambitious works of its kind ever to have been undertaken at that date. Wretchedly printed, probably in the interests of compressing as much information as possible into as short a space as possible, it is also of interest for the fact that it incorporated popular illustrative material in the form of frequent woodcuts. As with books printed throughout Europe at this time and earlier, each illustration was used several times throughout the book's course, a funeral scene for instance being used to supplement the records of funerals of successive monarchs, regardless of historical accuracy in matters such as costume and transport. Holinshed's work also incorporated an introductory section by William Harrison describing Elizabethan England, which is

Queene Eliza- beth.

present are certainly certified, that God this present morning hath called to his mercie, our late soueraigne Ladie Queene Marie, which happe as it is most heauie and grieuous vnto vs, so haue we no lesse cause an other way to reioyce, wyth prayse to almightie God, for that he hath left vnto vs a true, lawfull and right inheritrice to the crowne of this realme, which is the Ladie Elizabeth, second daughter to our late soueraigne Lord of noble memorie King Henrie the eight, and sister to our sayd late Queene, of whose most lawfull right and title in the succession of the crowne (thankes be to God) wee neede not to doubt. Wherefore the Lordes of this house haue determined with your assentes and consents, to passe from hence into the Palace, and there to proclaim the sayde Ladie Elizabeth Queene of thys realme, without further tract of tyme, wherevnto the whole house answered with euident apparaunce of ioy, God saue Queene Elizabeth, long may Queene Elizabeth raigne ouer vs: and so this present Parliament beeing dissolued by the acte of God, the sayde Lordes immediately calling vnto them the Kings and Principall Herauldes at Armes, went into the Palayce of Westmynster, and directly before the Hall dore in the fore Noone of the same day, after seuerall soundings of trumpets made, in most solemne maner proclamed the newe Queene, by thys name and tytle, *Elizabeth by the grace of God Queene of England, Fraunce and Irelande, defender of the fayth, &c.* to the great comfort and reioysing of the people, as by theyr maners and countenaunces well appeared, after which Proclamation made at Westminster, the sayde lords to witte the Duke of Norffolke, the Lord Treasurer, the Erle of Oxford, and diuerse other lords and Bishops, with all speede repayred into the Citie of London, where the lyke proclamation was made in presence of them, and also of the lord Maior and Aldermen in their skarlet gownes, at the Crosse in Cheape, with no lesse vniuersall ioy and thanks giuing to God of all the hearers: and so our sayd most gracious soueraigne Ladie Q. Elizabeth began hir happie raigne ouer this realm of Englande, to the great comfort and gladnesse of al estates, vpon the foresaid. xvij. day of Nouember, in the yere after the creation of the world. 5525. after the birth of our sauiour. 1558. of the Empire of Ferdinando the first Emperor of Rome bearing that name, the fyrste. In the. rij. pere of the raigne of Henrie the second of that name French King, and in the. rvj. yeare of the raigne of Marie Q. of Scotlande.

The Fryday morning being the. rviii. of Nouember, and morrow after the deceasse of Q. Marie, Reginalde Poole, Lorde Cardinall, and Archbishop of Canterburie departed this life et

Hen true knowledge was had ẏ Queene Mary was deceassed, who left hir life in this worlde the xvij. day of Nouember as is before mentioned in the latter ende of hir hystorie, in the tyme of a Parliament, the Lordes that were assembled in the vpper house, being resolued according to the lawes of the lande, to declare the Ladie Elizabeth sister to the sayde Queene to be verie true and lawfull heyre to the Crowne of Englande, sent immediately to the speaker of the Parliament, willing him with the knightes and Burgesses of the neather house, without delay to repayre vnto them into the vpper house, for their assents in a case of great importaunce: who being come thither, after silence made (as the maner is) the Archbishop of Yorke Chauncellor of Englande, whose name was Nicholas Heth, Doctor in Diuinitie, stood vp and pronounced in effect these wordes following.

The cause of your calling hither at this time, is to signifie vnto you, that all the Lordes here

A specimen page from Holinshed's Chronicles, *illustrating the beginning of the section devoted to Elizabeth I's reign.*

161

K

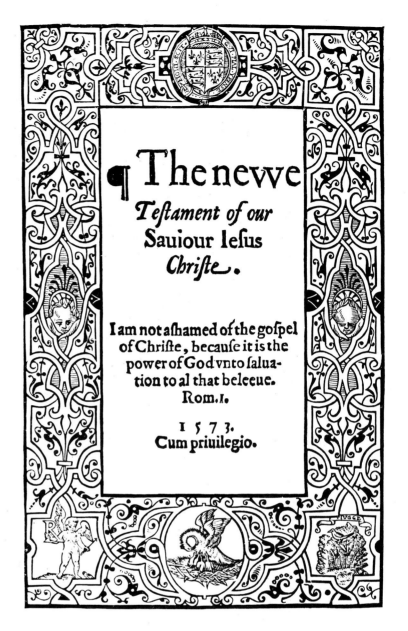

still of great value to historians. Works of this kind, as with laudatory poetry, tended to idealise Elizabeth and her reign; even so their value at the time of publication was high.

Although William Camden's most enduring work was his *Britannia*, an antiquarian survey in Latin of Great Britain, like Harrison's survey his *Annales* were written solely as a record of his own times. Born in London in 1551, Camden began teaching at Westminster School in 1575, and it was while he was there that he wrote his *Britannia*. The book was first published in 1586 and rapidly achieved popularity; presumably in part because of his resulting eminence Camden was appointed headmaster of Westminster in 1592, being created Clarenceux King of Arms in 1596. Later he became a professor of history at Oxford. He died in 1623, being buried in Westminster Abbey, assured long before that date of the acclamation of posterity.

John Stow, famous for his *Chronicles of England* and his *Survey of London*, was another of that breed of Elizabethan writer who relished the recording of accumulated facts. His book on London has subsequently become a classic, much of its information being unobtainable elsewhere in contemporary form. Naturally Stow's books, like others already mentioned, were intended only for an extremely limited readership, and in part because of this they were written not only as chronicles but also as literature, something quite different from the pragmatism and contumely of the numerous pamphlets that were such a feature of the Elizabethan publishing scene, each succeeding matter of dispute prompting a pamphlet war.

Camden's Britannia. *Here is shown the title page of the 1590 edition, revised and slightly enlarged over the original 1586 edition.*

Other books of an historical kind published during Elizabeth's reign had far different motives. John Foxe, author of what is usually known as *The Book of Martyrs* but was originally cloaked beneath the more sedate title of *Actes and Monuments*, published his great work in 1563. Again, Foxe was chronicling recent events, but his principal concern was to outline the severity of Mary I's attitude towards 'heretics'. He recorded the heresies of each of the martyrs of her reign and described in particularly gory detail the agonies of their executions.

On an entirely different level was the *Poly Olbion* of Michael Drayton. This consists of an extended poem, the first part of which was not published until 1613, describing England as it appeared to the poet in the age of Elizabeth. Like many of his contemporaries, Drayton was guilty of inordinate length in his writing, but his poem provides valuable topographical information nevertheless and was extremely popular at the time of publication. His desire to record factual information as completely as possible in his chosen field and manner equated with the practices of more conventional chroniclers.

This, then, represented one side of publishing during Elizabeth's reign. The publication of successful stage plays, adulatory poems (frequently anonymous and in anthologised form) represented another. And of course the printing of new editions and impressions of the Bible and prayer book provided 'stationers' with a considerable industry. All in all it was a flourishing period. Many thousands of books and pamphlets are recorded as having been published in England in Elizabeth's time, all of which were required to be registered at Stationers' Hall, the meeting place of the Stationers' Guild. These records have survived and have been published, and they make fascinating reading.

The Arts under Elizabeth

> *. . . a hand, or eye*
> *By* Hilliard *drawne, is worth an history,*
> *By a worse painter made.*

(John Donne: 'The Storm').

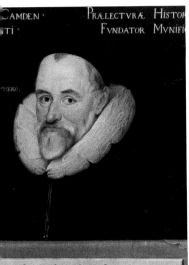

above:

William Camden, the great historian of Elizabeth's reign; a portrait attributed to Gheeraerts and now in the possession of the Bodleian Library at Oxford. The inscription in the lower half of the painting refers to Camden's two principal works, the Britannia *and the* Annales. *Gheeraerts the younger was probably the most accomplished painter active in England towards the end of the sixteenth century and beginning of the seventeenth century, having travelled from Flanders at an early age.*

Elizabeth I loved nothing more than to dance, and throughout her life indulged in this pastime. Her court echoed to the sound of music, and it was not surprising therefore that musical composition flourished during her reign. It was not in the field of dance and song, or even incidental music designed to accompany banquets and other festivities, that this art form flourished exclusively during the sixteenth century. Church music too felt the Renaissance influence.

The Anglican William Byrd stands supreme in this department of composition, his masses, motets and other sacred works possessing a daring freshness that for their time constituted something quite revolutionary. Byrd had naturally been influenced by such great continental masters as Palestrina —

who directed sacred music away from mere plainsong almost singlehanded — but his own contribution was both singular and lovely. A fine organist, Byrd had numerous competitors in England, most of them Roman Catholics. Thomas Tallis was probably second to him in achievement, though such works as his twelve-part motet, which is often heard today, are perhaps more deeply rooted in tradition than certain of Byrd's compositions.

If the sacred compositions of Elizabethan composers sometimes seem a little arcane today, almost without exception the popular songs and dance tunes of refined Elizabethan England still preserve their liveliness. The spirit of the age comes down to us in the suites, galliards and songs of such composers as Weelkes, Morley and the more subdued Dowland. The words of some of these songs also echo the spirit of the age, many of them embodying themes based upon such lines as 'Long live Fair Oriana', a reference to the queen. Orlando Gibbons, perhaps better known for his church music, nicely reflected another aspect of the Elizabethan character in his beautiful short song of 'The Silver Swan', which ends philosophically:

> *More geese than swans now live,*
> *More fools than wise.*

Musical instruments in use during Elizabeth's time ranged from keyboard instruments such as the spinet to the viola da gamba and other members of the viol family (a 'chest of viols' could consist of up to six different viols contained in one chest and normally played in concert). The lute, predecessor of the

Miniature painting in Elizabethan times reached a pitch of high excellence. The Frenchman Issac Oliver, who painted this miniature about 1595, was the equal of Nicholas Hilliard in this difficult art form. Now entitled 'A Melancholy Young Man', at one time this was thought to be a portrait of the poet and courtier Sir Philip Sidney, but this ascription is now very much in doubt. Author of a number of exquisite melancholy poems, Sidney could well have provided the subject for such a painting.

Elizabeth I on a picnic. Taken from Turberville's Book of Hunting *of 1575.*

guitar, was also a favoured instrument, and there were numerous members of the woodwind family. Queen Elizabeth was herself an accomplished musician, and a great patron of this art form; and although England has perhaps never produced the incidence of great musicians to have come from the main European continent, she at any rate achieved a good deal during the sixteenth century.

In the field of sculpture too England has rarely rivalled continental countries, though many of the church effigies of the middle ages and beyond surely rank as great works of art. In painting, however, England has always claimed an honourable place, and during the Elizabethan era a peculiarly English art form flourished that reached a high degree of excellence. This was of course miniature painting, with Nicholas Hilliard and Isaac Oliver emerging as the supreme exponents of this difficult craft. Elizabeth and her courtiers were frequently portrayed in this medium.

This was not the only form of pictorial art to achieve memorable standards during Elizabeth's reign. Life-size portraiture, allegorical painting and even the species of painting that could be loosely defined as reportage flourished admirably. The rich court clothes worn by the ladies and gentlemen of the time are depicted in all their intricate wealth of decorative luxuriance, and throughout this publication numerous illustrations show this trait in force. Figures are however usually portrayed very formally, while often enough facial features seem to bear the mark of distant contemplation, even melancholy. Why this should have been the case in the late sixteenth century is hard to ascertain, but this formal aspect of painting, together with the tendency to record every detail, may perhaps be likened to those literary chronicles mentioned elsewhere which aimed at recording everything for posterity. Details of dress, even details of foodstuffs included in domestic paintings, yield valuable information to the historian; equestrian paintings tell one much of riding and hunting habits and techniques, while depictions of military actions are full of irreplaceable information concerning naval and military matters of their age.

This is one aspect of Elizabethan painting. Expression of personal character in portraiture, even beneath the mask of formality, often surprises one, while in just a few instances, in the backgrounds of certain paintings, can be glimpsed the beginnings of English landscape painting. As was the case earlier in the century, many of the important painters working in England were of foreign birth, but such artists as George Gower and John Bettes were wholly English.

Of all the arts, however, literature has always been England's great glory, and no other nation can equal her in this. In Elizabethan times it flourished magnificently — even though the most significant writer of all happened to be a playwright. The novel was born during this era, in the work of Thomas Deloney, whose *Jack of Newberie* has still something more than purely antiquarian interest. Humorous writers also abounded, including Robert Greene and Thomas Nash. Epic poetry held its own, represented by Edmund Spenser (whose *Fairie Queene* clearly mirrored the gloriousness affected by the queen) and others, while first-rate translations from the Greek and Latin classics became almost an Elizabethan industry. Playwriting, historical writing and all other literary pursuits received royal patronage but it is probably in the field of poetry in its lighter vein (humorous poetry and amorous poetry) that Elizabethan literature is today best represented. One of the principal accomplishments of the Elizabethan gentleman was the ability to write verse, and thus it is that much of what has survived of this kind of verse was written by 'gentlemen amateurs'. Not in vain however is the age described more often than not, when referring to poetry, as the 'silver age'. Perhaps one of the most pleasing of all the lighter poems to have been written at this time, and one that reflects the musical interests of the age is from a manuscript anthology known as *Songs and Sonnets* dating from 1557. It is the work of Sir Thomas Wyatt (whose son led the Wyatt uprising of Mary's reign, mentioned elsewhere), and the first and last stanzas are quoted:

> My lute, awake! perform the last
> Labour that thou and I shall waste,
> And end that I have now begun;
> For when this song is sung and past,
> My lute, be still, for I have done.
>
> . . .
>
> Now cease, my lute! this is the last
> Labour that thou and I shall waste,
> And ended is that we begun;
> Now is this song both sung and past.
> My lute, be still, for I have done.

The Great Seal of Westminster Abbey, 1560, showing Elizabeth on one side and the abbey's founder, Edward the Confessor, on the other.

overleaf:

The delightful painting illustrated here of Lord and Lady Cobham and their family, attributed to Hans Eworth, shows one of Elizabeth's principal ministers in a domestic surrounding. He is portrayed together with his wife, sister and six children and the painter's skill has well recorded the dress of this comfortably off aristocratic family, especially that of the children, all of whom are extravagantly attired and made to look as much as possible like miniature adults. The Dutchman Eworth flourished in England between 1540 and 1573. Today he is held by many to have been one of the most important painters active during his time. He acquired fame and patronage when Mary I adopted him as her official portraitist. When Elizabeth succeeded to the throne Eworth lost his royal patronage for a time; however, in 1572 the new queen commissioned him to provide decorations and costume designs for court fetes.

igna . parente . cohors
patriarchae menfa . Iacobi .
c . cumulata . pio .
haec . gignat menfa . Iofephi
irps . renouata . fuit ;
onafti . laeta . Cobhamo
os . gaudia . tanta . dies :
· 1 5 6 7 ·

SVAE 5 GEMELLI

AETA 4

The Spanish question

The Queen's Majesty is credibly informed that sundry persons of good wealth and calling having their habitation within sundry shires bordering upon the seacoast have of late time departed from their said houses and part of them withdrawn themselves from their houses on the seacoasts, and some other part out of the maritime counties into inland counties, and many of them to the city of London or to places near about; whereby not only the accustomed hospitality in those places but specially the ability and strength for defense of those counties are notably decayed; whereof her majesty, in respect of her royal estate and dignity, to whom the special charge hereof belongeth, cannot but give order and provide speedy remedy for the same.

And therefore her majesty chargeth and commandeth, upon pain of her highness' indignation, besides such forfeiture of their lands and goods as justly by her authority royal they may incur, that every person of any degree that

Design for a tapestry commemorating the English victory over the Spanish Armada.

hath within these two years next passed before the last Feast of Michaelmas had habitation in any county that bordereth upon the sea shall, if he be there, so continue his habitation; and if he have removed from his said habitation to any place more distant from the sea within the said two years, then he shall . . . without delay return to his said former habitation, and within one month after the publication hereof in the said county shall stable his household in the said former place with such number of servants, or more, as before time were there kept. . . .

(Proclamation by Elizabeth I, Richmond, November 2, 1587).

The year 1588 is remembered by every Englishman: in that year English ships established English naval supremacy in European waters, beating off and partly destroying the invading Spanish Armada. Although Elizabeth had by that time been thirty years on the throne and the Spanish question had occupied her thoughts throughout her reign, the initial impetus to this particular crisis sprang ostensibly from a date not long before the launching of the Armada itself, from 1585. In that year Spain intimated to Rome that a religious war might be begun against Elizabeth, in order to re-establish Catholicism as the official English religion and to rout out those who were firmly opposed to Rome. Among other excuses given by Philip II to justify his invasion at this time was the hoped for restoration to the Scottish throne of Queen Mary. These were Philip's expressed aims, together with certain other well-meaning intentions. His unexpressed aim was to ensure that, should Elizabeth be murdered or otherwise vacate the throne, the English crown would fall into the hands of somebody who would prove helpful towards himself. Philip incurred Pope Sixtus V's deserved scepticism, but the following year he nevertheless succeeded in extracting the promise of 1,000,000 crowns from the Vatican to assist him in his cause — half of it payable following the landing of a Spanish army on English shores, the remainder periodically thereafter.

171

In 1587, while Mary, Queen of Scots, was still alive, Philip attempted to persuade the Vatican to declare that if ultimately Mary proved unable to assume the English throne it should pass to Philip himself, out of recognition of his having at one time been joint ruler of England (as husband of Mary I). The Pope would give no answer to this proposition, deferring the matter until such time as Spain had succeeded in conquering England. In the meantime Mary was executed.

Philip made copious plans for the invasion of England, taking the advice of his brilliant admiral, Santa Cruz, but finally having to abandon the admiral's scheme for a combined naval and military invasion in deference to its prohibitive cost. Utilising the army of Parma and assuming some support from the English Catholics, Philip began publicly planning the invasion as early as the close of 1585, assembling his troops and fitting out his ships (which rallied in Cadiz harbour), England herself taking preliminary steps to meet this force by the middle of the year following.

During the spring of 1587 Drake was ordered to set sail and harass the Spanish fleet as much as possible, eventually penetrating Cadiz harbour and wreaking considerable havoc. Among Drake's other achievements at this juncture was the destruction of Santa Cruz' galleon and the consequent capture of much treasure. He challenged the Spaniards to a full naval encounter, but they would not meet him. Returning home after almost two and a half months, Drake had the satisfaction of knowing that he had at any rate delayed the promised invasion for a good twelve months. Philip had to begin his preparations all over again, the intelligence of his plans and progress spreading almost as rapidly as they were achieved.

The Spanish monarch then faced a series of catastrophes. Troops previously available to him in the Netherlands were reduced through death from 30,000 to 17,000; then in February, 1588 Santa Cruz died, being replaced by the Duke of Medina Sidonia. Medina Sidonia knew nothing of sea warfare, had been

Here the two fleets are seen off the English coast near the Isle of Wight, on July 25, 1588. The Spanish fleet is on the left, the English on the right; both are becalmed with their sails furled.

selected arbitrarily and was very much against his task. He finally set sail at the head of an invasion force at the end of May, 1588, England being fully prepared to repulse him, confident of her ability to destroy the Spaniards at sea (though Philip probably enjoyed superiority on land, and the outcome to his invasion may well have been very different had his troops been able to effect a landing).

Philip had worked carefully over his plans for a sea encounter, and hoped initially to lure the English ships, under the command of Lord Howard of Effingham, close to his own; secondary to this was a plan to capture the Isle of Wight for use as a base in the future should the present campaign prove less than successful and the Duke of Parma's troops be unable to cross the Channel in support of the invading Armada (the heavy ships of Medina Sidonia being incapable of approaching his ports of departure and providing the necessary protection to the smaller craft). The English force consisted of a grand fleet of sixteen ships under Howard, based in the Thames at Queenborough, a squadron of light craft under Sir Henry Palmer, based at Dover, and Sir Francis Drake's small scout force at Plymouth. In May, 1588 Howard and his fleet joined Drake at Plymouth, full details of the Spanish strength then being known.

Thereafter England did not show any inclination to seize the initiative that her information would certainly have afforded. The obvious course would have been to set sail and engage the Spaniards in their own waters, as far away from England as possible, hoping that Palmer's fleet at Dover would be sufficient to repulse the troops of Parma if they did attempt to cross the channel. The reason for the delay was based on Elizabeth's firm belief that peace could be achieved without resort to arms (until the middle of June her ambassadors were discussing this possibility in Brussels with the Duke of Parma).

Once the talks with Parma were concluded Howard was authorised to put to sea, which he did during the final week of June. He received intimation that the

Spanish fleet was undergoing repair along the Biscay coast, having suffered from gales when it put to sea at the end of May. Had the winds not also attacked Howard (introducing the danger of being stranded without provisions on the coast of Spain) he would undoubtedly have despatched the Spanish fleet at that time; instead he returned to England.

On July 12 the Spanish fleet emerged from Corunna, sighting Cornwall one week later. Beacons were lit along the English coast and Howard's force put out of Plymouth. The two engaged on July 21. Virtually uninterrupted battle then raged for ten days; the Spanish fleet, however, continued up the Channel, Howard succeeding in inflicting only minor damage, not chancing a full offensive until his entire fleet had rallied. For the first week the Spaniards appeared the stronger of the two fleets; only on July 28 did the English gain the upper hand, when Howard caused eight ships coated with pitch to be set alight and let loose among the Spanish craft. This caused confusion enough, but it also prompted a full-scale engagement the following day, the Battle of Gravelines, the turning point in the war, when the Spanish fleet was suddenly placed in grave danger of total destruction.

Medina Sidonia sped away towards Dunkirk, the insistent gunnery of the English inflicting continual damage to his ships. Then, on July 30, the wind shifted to such an extent that the Spanish were in danger of being driven onto the Ruytingen shoals. With five ships out of action and two others completely wrecked, the fleeing admiral was in very serious difficulties indeed. The wind changed just in time and he was able to escape into the North Sea. He then steered a course for home by navigating around the British Isles; Howard pursued him as far as the Firth of Forth before resting, satisfied that victory was his.

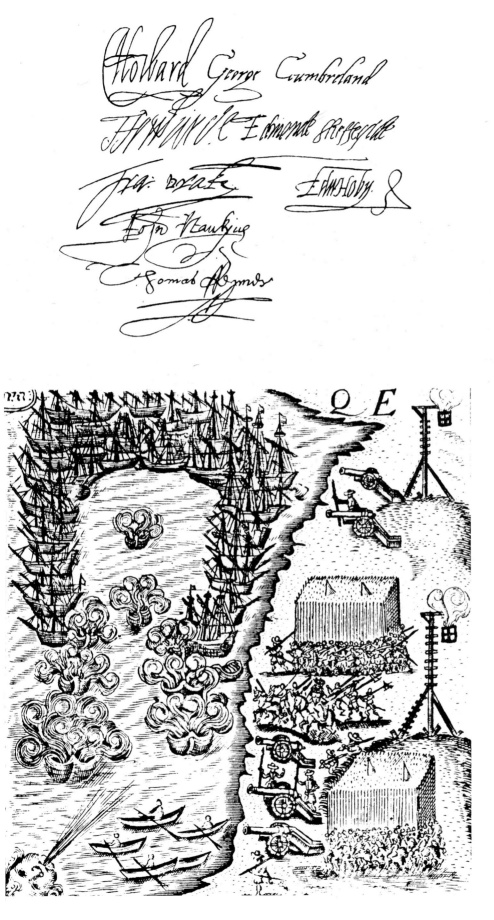

The signatures of the English leaders against the Spanish Armada.

In this old woodcut the launching of the fireships can be plainly seen, but more significant is the presence of the English queen on horseback, encouraging her troops at Tilbury.

Following the Armada's defeat Elizabeth and many of her subjects gave thanks in St. Paul's Cathedral, on November 24, 1588.

The protracted engagement and subsequent pursuit naturally meant that intelligence of the outcome was prevented from reaching Spain, and tales actually filtered through not only that victory had gone to Medina Sidonia but that the English had suffered severe losses. It was even rumoured in certain places that Spanish troops had landed in England. However, the truth of her disaster eventually reached Spain about the beginning of September; while Medina Sidonia, who was still on the way home, lost further ships in the Irish Sea and gained Spain with a much reduced and very battered fleet, many of his surviving men sick or wounded. His total loss was in the region of 63 ships, about half his strength. Only two of these were actually known to have sunk during the principal engagement with the English, while the frightful number of nineteen is recorded as perishing off Scotland and Ireland on the homeward voyage. The English lost not one ship.

The end of Elizabeth's reign

Be always faithful to me, as I always desire to keep you in peace; and if there have been wiser kings, none has ever loved you more than I have.

(Elizabeth I at the age of 67 in 1601).

It is something of a tragedy that the closing years of Elizabeth's reign should have proved something of an anti-climax. With the Tudor line coming to an end it seemed as though misfortune must dog the final years of its ascendancy. Political troubles connected with foreign matters had occupied Elizabeth throughout her reign, and so it was hardly surprising that these should continue; but that troubles much closer to the throne, in the form of a rather farcical rebellion, should cause concern was a sorry indignity. Elizabeth continued to make progresses, displaying her person in all regnal splendour; travel, discovery and overseas trade continued to flourish, culminating in 1599 with the founding of the East India Company; but somehow the essential glamour of Elizabeth's reign had gone.

Among the principal nautical enterprises of the latter half of the reign should be mentioned the voyage of Drake and Hawkins to the West Indies in 1595; but this also failed to achieve the success of earlier years. Seventeen ships and a complement of 2,500 men constituted the force of this expedition, whose purpose was to attack Spanish galleons bearing treasure and Spanish garrisons ashore. The English troops under Sir Thomas Baskerville were repulsed as they crossed the Panama isthmus, while both Hawkins and Drake perished on the expedition. Hawkins fell ill and was buried at sea off Porto Rico, while Drake

A naval engagement, from Holinshed's Chronicles.

IVDGE POPHAM

died of dysentry at Porto Bello. Baskerville returned to England the following year with only failure to report, and the inference was that the Spaniards, although they might have been trounced in English waters in 1588, held the whip hand in the Caribbean and south America.

The story of the East India Company was far happier. Little success had come from various westerly enterprises and so it was only logical to take advantage of known territories to the east, of India and the East Indies. In 1591, under the command of one James Lancaster, three ships travelled as far as Ceylon, returning to England three years later. It was the intelligence brought home by members of this expedition — many of whose fellows had died on voyage — that provided the impetus to commence trading with the east. Ralph Fitch, who is mentioned elsewhere in these pages, also provided encouragement when he returned from the east in the same year. Over £70,000 was quickly raised to start a trading company, and on December 31, 1599 the East India Company received its charter of incorporation. This consisted of a concession of fifteen years duration, granted to George Clifford, Earl of Cumberland, and some 215 others, to enjoy exclusive trading rights in the East Indies. In April, 1600 five ships sailed from Torbay to establish the company overseas, and for almost 300 years this company flourished, its power in India becoming ever more pronounced.

Ireland had always presented English monarchs with a problem. In 1599 Essex, much against his will, was given the virtually impossible task of solving the current Irish problem, being appointed Lord Lieutenant. His task, as had been the case with previous incumbents, was to pacify the two Irish factions, the southerners and the Ulstermen, and to subjugate the country to England. With fighting necessary on two fronts Essex' job was made doubly difficult. He did succeed in making a truce with the northern province, but he then made the error of returning to England, contrary to his orders, to seek the queen's advice and approval of what he had so far accomplished. Bursting in on the queen while she was still in her bedchamber, he made his explanation; but that same afternoon the queen and her council ruled that he should be held in custody pending a full enquiry. He was placed under the surveillance of the Lord Keeper, Sir Thomas Egerton, at York House.

Essex was now a sick man, and his cause was not helped by the breaking of the truce in Ulster. The queen added to his trouble by depriving him of his monopoly of sweet wines, which theretofore had provided him with the bulk of his income. He was kept prisoner for eight months and then brought before a commission. Stripped of all his offices, he was finally given his freedom on August 26, 1600.

It was now that Essex' so-called 'rebellion' flared; although this is a misnomer, for his intentions were to protect his queen rather than to overthrow her. In a hair-brained dash through the city of London at the head of only about 200 men, he tried to warn the citizens that the Spanish infanta, Clara Eugenia, was set to inherit the English crown on Elizabeth's death, and not James VI of Scotland whom he took to be the rightful heir. He had already attempted to raise troops in both Scotland and Ireland to assist him in preventing this catastrophe, and when he was finally obliged to surrender to the queen's men he must have known that his fate was sealed and that he would lose his head. This he did at the age of 33, the one-time favourite of a monarch who at the time was 67 years old. Rather than await the inevitable time when he would have regained his queen's favour, he had given way to self-indulgent panic, and it cost him his life. As far as Elizabeth herself was concerned, Essex' death could only have been something of a tragedy.

The fall of Essex was only one sign of the times. The ascendancy of Robert Cecil, Burghley's son, appointed Secretary of State in 1596, was another — for he acquired the reputation of being 'king' in England. But beyond this was the

opposite:
Sir John Popham, appointed Lord Chief Justice of the Common Pleas in 1592, at whose home at Littlecote in Wiltshire Elizabeth stayed in 1601. In the same year Popham was one of the accusers of Essex and his co-conspirators who were eventually executed for treason.

Robert, Earl of Essex.

gradual acceptance of the right of Roman Catholics to follow their own religion in England, on the understanding that they owed allegiance to the English throne in temporal matters, not to the Pope, whatever the circumstances. Elizabeth tried hard to oppose this new circumstance, but she could not stave its progress permanently. The fact was Elizabeth had become too set in her ways to allow for change. Advanced in age for her times, she could not hope to live for very much longer.

The end came on March 24, 1603. The queen had been ailing for two years, growing all the time more testy and isolated. In her sickness it became necessary to remove the ring from her finger which had symbolised her marriage to the realm of England, but it had to be filed through, so deeply embedded in her flesh had it become. Its removal heralded the end, and she travelled from Whitehall to Richmond, mainly in quest of more clement weather. She died there, and among her last words was the charge that her 'kinsman', James VI of Scotland, should succeed to the throne.

Thus the Tudor era came to a conclusion. The House of Stuart, albeit related to the Tudors, now came into power. With its coming an entirely new set of problems was destined to ensnare Englishmen and their leaders.

Family Tree
Chronology
and Acknowledgements

A Tudor Family Tree

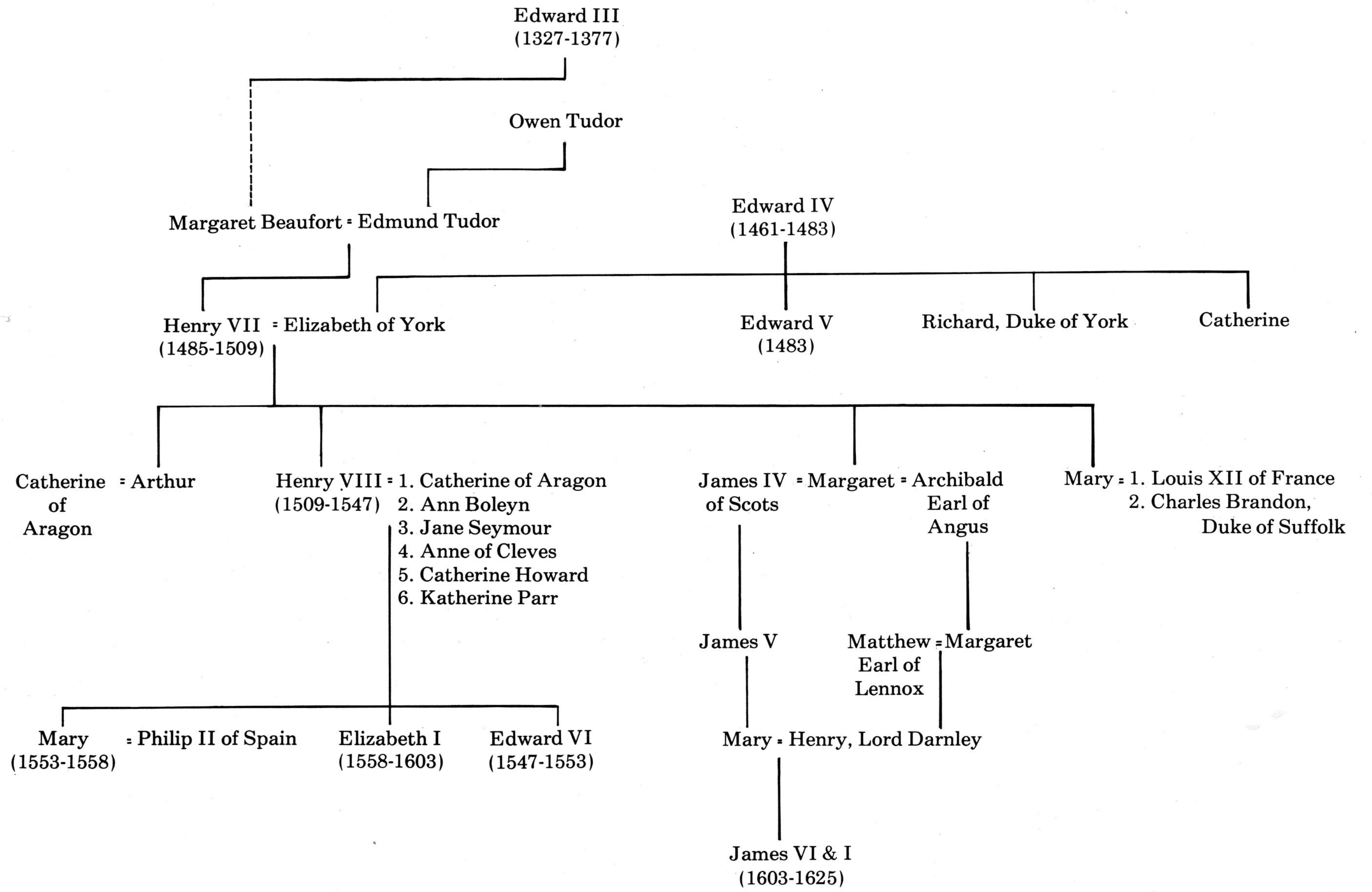

Edward III
(1327-1377)

Owen Tudor

Margaret Beaufort = Edmund Tudor

Edward IV
(1461-1483)

Richard, Duke of York

Catherine

Edward V
(1483)

Henry VII = Elizabeth of York
(1485-1509)

Catherine = Arthur
of
Aragon

Henry VIII = 1. Catherine of Aragon
(1509-1547)   2. Ann Boleyn
              3. Jane Seymour
              4. Anne of Cleves
              5. Catherine Howard
              6. Katherine Parr

James IV = Margaret = Archibald
of Scots   Earl of
                      Angus

Mary = 1. Louis XII of France
       2. Charles Brandon,
          Duke of Suffolk

James V

Matthew = Margaret
Earl of
Lennox

Mary = Philip II of Spain   Elizabeth I   Edward VI
(1553-1558)   (1558-1603)   (1547-1553)

Mary = Henry, Lord Darnley

James VI & I
(1603-1625)

182

Chronology

The Reign of Henry VII

Aug. 22, 1485	Richard III killed on Bosworth Field.
Nov. 7, 1485	Henry VII crowned.
1485	Malory's *Morte D'Arthur* printed and published by Caxton.
May 5, 1487	Yorkist rebellion.
Oct. 2, 1492	Henry VII lands in France.
Nov. 3, 1492	The Peace of Etaples.
1499	Erasmus settles at Oxford.
1501	First voyage of the Anglo-Portuguese syndicate to North America.
Apr. 2, 1502	Death of Arthur, Prince of Wales, at Ludlow.
Aug. 8, 1502	Margaret Tudor, Henry VII's daughter, marries James IV of Scotland.
1503	Parliament approves the Statute of Retainers.
1503	Henry VII's chapel, Westminster Abbey, begun (completed 1519).
1504	Henry VII places the guilds and companies under state control.
1505	Henry VII grants a new charter to the Merchant Adventurers.
Apr. 30, 1506	A commercial treaty signed between England and the Netherlands.
Mar. 23, 1509	Death of Henry VII; succeeded by his son, Henry VIII.

The Reign of Henry VIII

Jan.-Feb., 1510	Henry VIII granted tonnage, poundage and wool duties for the duration of his life by Parliament.
Oct. 4, 1511	An alliance formed against France between Henry VIII, Ferdinand, King of Aragon, and Pope Julius II.
1511	Erasmus' *In Praise of Folly* published.
Aug. 16, 1513	Henry VIII and the Emperor Maximilian I defeat the French in the 'Battle of Spurs'.
Aug. 6, 1514	Peace between England and France.
Feb. 2, 1522	Henry VIII granted the title 'Fidei Defensor' by Pope Leo X.
1525	William Tyndale translates the New Testament.
1525	Wolsey founds Cardinal College (later Christ Church), Oxford.
1526	Hans Holbein settles in England.
Apr. 30, 1527	Peace of Amiens between England and France.
Jan. 21, 1528	England declares war on France.
Oct. 17, 1529	Fall of Wolsey; succeeded by Thomas More October 25.
1530	English merchants in Spain formed into a company.
1530	The first of William Hawkins' three expeditions to Brazil.
Feb., 1531	Henry VIII recognised as the supreme head of the English Church.
1532	Publication of the first complete edition of Chaucer's works.
Jan. 25, 1533	Henry VIII marries Anne Boleyn secretly.
Mar. 30, 1533	Thomas Cranmer appointed Archbishop of Canterbury.
Apr. 12, 1533	Thomas Cromwell appointed a Privy Councillor and Secretary of State.
Apr. 23, 1533	Henry VIII's marriage to Catherine of Aragon declared void.
Jul. 11, 1533	Henry VIII excommunicated by Pope Clement VII.
Mar. 23, 1534	Henry VIII's marriage to Catherine of Aragon declared valid by Papal decree.
Aug. 15, 1534	The Act of Supremacy passed severing the English Church from that of Rome.
Jan., 1535	The English bishops abjure Papal authority.
Jan. 21, 1535	Henry VIII authorises the 'visitation' of English churches and monasteries.
Jul. 6, 1535	Thomas More beheaded.
1536	Unification of the English and Welsh systems of government.
1536	Dissolution of the lesser English monasteries.
1536	Reform of the universities.
May 19, 1536	Anne Boleyn beheaded.
May 30, 1536	Henry VIII marries Jane Seymour.
Jul. 2, 1536	Thomas Cromwell appointed Lord Privy Seal.

Jul. 18, 1536	The authority of the Bishop of Rome declared void for England.
1536-1537	The Pilgrimage of Grace.
1539	The dissolution of the greater monasteries.
1539	England grants merchants free trade for seven years.
May, 1539	Henry VIII issues his 'Six Articles'.
Jan. 6, 1540	Henry marries Anne of Cleves.
Jul. 6, 1540	Henry VIII's marriage to Anne of Cleves declared void.
Jul. 28, 1540	Henry marries Catherine Howard.
Jul. 29, 1540	Thomas Cromwell beheaded. Six new bishops created.
1541	John Knox begins the Reformation in Scotland.
1541	Henry VIII assumes the title of King of Ireland, also head of the Irish Church.
Feb. 13, 1542	Catherine Howard beheaded.
Jul. 12, 1542	Henry VIII marries Katherine Parr.
Jul., 1542	War between England and Scotland.
1542	Magdalene College, Cambridge, founded.
Nov. 24, 1542	Scots defeated at Solway Moss.
Dec. 8, 1542	Mary, Queen of Scots, born.
Dec. 14, 1542	James V of Scotland dies and Arran appointed regent for Mary.
Feb., 1543	Henry VIII allies with the Emperor Charles V against Francis I of France.
Jul. 1, 1543	The Peace of Greenwich between England and Scotland; engagement between Prince Edward (later Edward VI) and Mary, Queen of Scots.
Dec. 11, 1543	The Scottish Parliament repudiates the Treaty of Greenwich.
May, 1544	England invades Scotland; Leith and Edinburgh captured.
Jul., 1544	Henry VIII and Charles V take St. Dizier and threaten Paris.
Sep. 14, 1544	Henry VIII takes Boulogne.
Feb. 25, 1545	The Scots defeat the English at Ancrum Moor.
1546	Trinity College, Cambridge, founded.
1546	The English Navy Board established.
Jun. 7, 1546	Peace of Ardres between England and France: Boulogne to remain under English control for a period of eight years.
Jan. 28, 1547	Death of Henry VIII; succeeded by his son, Edward VI.

The Reign of Edward VI

Jan. 31, 1547	Somerset appointed Lord Protector.
Sep. 10, 1547	The Scots defeated at Pinkie.
1548	Religious guilds and chantries abolished (the Chantries Act).
Jun. 9, 1549	A period of social and religious unrest begins in Devon, Cornwall, Norfolk, Yorkshire. Enclosures are legalised and provision dealers are forbidden to act in concert to keep prices high.
Aug. 9, 1549	England declares war on France.
Jan., 1550	Somerset is deposed and succeeded by Northumberland.
Mar. 24, 1550	The Peace of Boulogne between France and England and between England and Scotland. England cedes Boulogne.
Jan., 1552	The second Act of Uniformity, and the second Prayer Book printed.
Jan. 22, 1552	Somerset beheaded.
Feb. 24, 1552	Hansa privileges abolished in England.
Jul. 6, 1553	Edward VI dies; succeeded by Mary I.

The Reign of Mary I

Aug.-Sep., 1553	The arrest of the Protestant bishops and the restoration of Roman Catholicism in England.
Feb. 12, 1554	Jane Grey beheaded.
Apr. 12, 1554	Mary of Lorraine succeeds Arran as Scots regent.
Jul. 25, 1554	Mary I marries Philip, later Philip II of Spain.
Nov. 30, 1554	England is reconciled with Rome and Roman Catholicism is fully restored.
Oct. 16, 1555	Bishops Ridley and Latimer burnt at Oxford.
Mar. 21, 1556	Cranmer is burnt, and the following day Pole becomes Archbishop of Canterbury.
Jun. 7, 1557	England declares war on France.
Aug. 10, 1557	England and Spain defeat France at St. Quentin.
Apr. 24, 1558	Mary, Queen of Scots, marries the Dauphin Francis.
Nov. 17, 1558	Mary I dies; succeeded by Elizabeth I.

The Reign of Elizabeth I

Nov. 20, 1558	William Cecil appointed Chief Secretary of State.
Jun. 22, 1559	Elizabeth I's Prayer Book issued.
Aug., 1559	Parker created Archbishop of Canterbury.
Feb. 27, 1560	Treaty of Berwick between the Scottish Lords and Elizabeth I.
Jul. 6, 1560	Treaty of Edinburgh between England and Scotland.
Aug. 19, 1561	Mary, Queen of Scots, lands in Scotland.
1562	John Hawkins begins the slave trade between Africa and America.
Sep. 20, 1562	Treaty of Hampton Court between Elizabeth I and the Huguenots.
Oct., 1562	The English occupy Le Havre.
Jul. 28, 1563	Le Havre recaptured by the French during the Huguenot War.
1563	Foxe's *Book of Martyrs* published.
1564	Trade war between England and Spain. Philip II confiscates English ships.
Apr. 11, 1564	Anglo-French Peace at Troyes.
1564	Hawkins begins his second voyage to South America.
Jul. 29, 1565	Mary, Queen of Scots, marries Darnley.
Feb. 10, 1567	Darnley murdered.
May 15, 1567	Mary, Queen of Scots, marries Bothwell.
Jul. 24, 1567	Mary, Queen of Scots, abdicates.
May 13, 1568	Mary, Queen of Scots, defeated at Langside. Flees to England on May 19.
Sep., 1568	The English defeated by the Spaniards off the Mexican coast.
Feb. 25, 1571	Cecil created Lord Burghley.
Apr.-May, 1571	Parliament forbids the importation of Papal Bulls into England.
1571	Convocation sanctions the Thirty Nine Articles.
1572	Drake attacks Spanish harbours in America.
1572	Embargo against England by the Spanish Netherlands.
Jul., 1572	Burghley appointed Lord High Treasurer.
Feb. 11, 1573	Drake sees the Pacific from the Isthmus of Panama.
1575	Sir Humphrey Gilbert's *Discourse* published, advocating English colonisation.
Jul., 1576	Frobisher annexes Frobisher Bay, off Baffin Island.
1576	Three theatres built in London.
1577	Frobisher's second voyage. A general patent of colonisation granted to Gilbert.
1577	Ralph Holinshed's *Chronicles* published.
1578	Frobisher's third voyage.
1579	Spenser's *Shepherd's Calendar* published.
1579	Gilbert's expedition to the West Indies fails.
1579	England withdraws Hanseatic privileges.

Jun. 17, 1579	Drake establishes English possession of California ('New Albion').
1580	Lyly's *Euphues* published.
1580	First commercial treaty between England and Turkey.
1581	An Act introduced to impose heavy fines on Catholic recusants.
1581	Sidney's *Arcadia* published.
1582	James VI of Scotland falls into the hands of the English.
1582	Hakluyt's *Voyages* published.
Aug., 1583	Gilbert founds the first colony in Newfoundland, but does not establish it by patent.
1584	Raleigh annexes Newfoundland.
Nov., 1584	Parliament passes bills against plotters; Jesuits and seminary priests are expelled.
1585	Leicester takes English troops to Holland to support the Dutch against the French.
1585	Shakespeare leaves Stratford for London.
1585	John Davis begins his voyage in quest of the north-west passage; he discovers instead the Davis Strait, to the west of Greenland.
Oct. 14-15, 1586	Trial of Mary, Queen of Scots.
1586	Cavendish begins the third circumnavigation of the world.
1586	Camden's *Britannia* published.
1587	Second English settlement of Virginia (fails in 1591).
Feb. 8, 1587	Mary, Queen of Scots, beheaded.
Apr. 19, 1587	English expedition under Drake attacks Cadiz.
1588	Charter granted to the English Guinea Company.
Jul. 31-Aug. 8, 1588	Spanish Armada defeated.
1590	Parts I-III of Spenser's *Fairie Queene* published.
1590	Marlowe's *Tamburlaine* first acted.
1591	Shakespeare's *Henry VI* first acted.
1591	First English voyage to the East Indies by Lancaster.
1592	Marlowe's *Faustus* first published.
1593	Shakespeare's *Richard III* and *Comedy of Errors* both first acted.
1593	Marlowe killed.
Feb., 1593	Parliament passes an Act against 'seditious sectaries and disloyal persons'.
May 29, 1593	Opponents of Royal supremacy executed.
Feb. 21, 1595	The Jesuit poet Robert Southwell hanged.
1597	Shakespeare's *Romeo and Juliet* first acted.
Aug. 1, 1597	English merchants and goods banished from the Hanseatic territories.
1598	Stow's *Survey of London* published.
Aug. 4, 1598	Death of Burghley.
1599	Essex appointed Lord Lieutenant of Ireland; in the following year a new rising in County Tyrone.
Dec. 31, 1599	The East India Company established.

Apr., 1600	William Adams lands in Japan.
Feb. 13, 1601	East India Company ships sail for the first time, under Lancaster.
1602	Bodleian Library opened.
1603	*Hamlet* acted for the first time.
Apr. 10, 1603	Elizabeth I dies; James VI of Scotland proclaimed King of England, Scotland, France and Ireland.

Acknowledgements

Grateful acknowledgement of copyright for illustrations is made as follows: —

By Gracious Permission of Her Majesty the Queen, Portrait of a Young Man by Isaac Oliver; Henry, Lord Darnley and his brother by Eworth; Arthur, Prince of Wales by an unknown artist; The embarkation of Henry VIII for the Field of the Cloth of Gold by an unknown artist; The Field of the Cloth of Gold by an unknown artist; Elizabeth I as a Princess, c.1547, by an unknown artist; Edward VI by an unknown artist; Henry VII and his family, c.1508, by an unknown artist; the shield presented to Henry VIII by Francis I, said to be by Cellini.

The Archbishop of Canterbury (copyright reserved by the Courtauld Institute of Art and the Church Commissioners) the painting of Katherine Parr by an unknown artist.

The Mansell Collection, The noble array of the Armada; Engagement of the Fleet off 'Poortlant'; A Thankful Remembrance; English and Spanish fleets off Dunne Nose; Queen Elizabeth sitting in Judgement on the Pope; Queen Elizabeth hunting; The pond at Elvetham; A Royal Picnic.

The National Portrait Gallery, London, the paintings of Anne Boleyn; Catherine of Aragon; Mary, Queen of Scots; Wolsey; Thomas More; Thomas Cromwell; Mary I; Cranmer; Latimer; Sir Francis Drake; Elizabeth of York; Elizabeth I; Lady Jane Dudley (Grey); Philip II of Spain.

The British Museum, Henry VIII Supremacy of the Church medal; Thomas Cromwell medal; Edward VI Coronation medal; Silver Medal of Drake's voyage, 1586; Henry VIII sovereign; Mary I 'Royal'; Henry VIII's handwriting in 1518; Catherine of Aragon's handwriting; Henry VIII at his Devotions; Henry VIII playing the harp; Thomas Cranmer's handwriting; Mary I's handwriting; Signatures of the English leaders against the Armada; Elizabeth I's handwriting.

Crown Copyright, reproduced with the permission of the Controller of Her Majesty's Stationery Office, Portions of Henry VIII's armour; grotesque helmet; Astronomical clock at Hampton Court; Portrait of Anne of Cleves.

The Worshipful Company of Barbers, A 'Grace Cup'.

The Victoria and Albert Museum, Henry VII by Torrigiano; Henry VIII's writing desk; The Oxburgh Hangings; Carved panelling from a house at Waltham Abbey.

The Ashmolean Museum, Oxford, Queen Elizabeth I's riding boots; The steel band that fastened Cranmer to the stake.

The National Maritime Museum, Greenwich, An astrolabe of 1588; The launching of the fireships against the Armada; Armada tapestry design.

Mrs Elizabeth Brocklehurst, Sudeley Castle, the paintings of the Marriage of Henry VII; Mary Tudor; The three children of Henry VII; Thomas, Lord Seymour; Sir Francis Walsingham; The Lord Protector Somerset.

The Viscount De L'Isle, V.C., K.G., from his collection at Penshurst Place, Kent, Elizabeth I dancing with the Earl of Leicester.

G.A.G. Howard, Esq, Castle Howard, the painting of Henry VIII, by Holbein.

The Marquess of Bath, Longleat House, the paintings of Robert Devereux, Earl of Essex and of Lord and Lady Cobham and family.

Simon Wingfield-Digby, Esq, Sherborne Castle, the painting of Elizabeth I progressing.

The Bodleian Library, Oxford (Photos Nicholas Servian, Woodmansterne Limited) for portraits of Sir Martin Frobisher by Ketel and the portrait of William Camden, attributed to Gheeraerts.

The Master, the Lord Leycester Hospital, Warwick, portrait of Robert Dudley, Earl of Leicester.

The Marquess of Exeter, Burghley House, William Cecil, Lord Burghley by Gheeraerts; Burghley House; the canopy of Elizabeth I's bed.

David Seton Wills, Esq, Littlecote House, portrait of Sir John Popham.

Mary Evans Picture Library, Richmond Palace; Sebastian Cabot; Henry VIII; The Pope surpressed by Henry VIII; Henry VIII in old age; Latimer preaching; The martyrdom of Ridley and Latimer; Matthew Parker; Sir John Hawkins; Sir Humphrey Gilbert; The Globe Theatre; Ben Johnson.

For certain of the black and white illustrations, compiler and publisher are deeply indebted to the librarian of the *London Library*, who kindly allowed photographs to be taken from volumes in his care.

Author and publisher have made every attempt to secure reproduction rights of the illustrations contained in this book and apologise in advance for any accidental infringement that might have taken place.